REGISTRARS ON RECORD

Essays on Museum Collections Management

MARY CASE, EDITOR

A PUBLICATION OF THE REGISTRARS COMMITTEE
OF THE AMERICAN ASSOCIATION OF MUSEUMS

American Association of Museums
1225 Eye Street, N.W.
Suite 200
Washington, D.C. 20005

Table of Contents

Contents

Introduction

Acknowledgments

This book was Karol Schmiegel's idea. In August of 1984, she and I, Cordelia Rose, and Donna DeSalvo met for lunch to talk through Karol's plans as recently elected chairwoman of the Registrars Committee of the American Association of Museums (AAM). She proposed a book as a way to commemorate the 1986 tenth anniversary of the committee. She accomplished much during her tenure but nothing, I imagine, required more sustained guidance than this book.

David Wright and Eleanor Mish helped to draft the initial list of topics and a series of questions we eventually sent to the membership for response. We intended to use these responses as personal bridges between the topics but because of the way the book evolved, the replies don't appear verbatim on the following pages. Instead, the answers informed the process and influenced the outline revealed in the essays. Those who took the time to answer on three-by-five-inch index cards (as instructed) will, I hope, be cheered to know that their answers have been carefully placed in the Registrars Committee archives and that these often touching and poignant words sustained me through many late nights of word-smithing and ebbs in process. These registrars are: Eloise Ricciardelli, Judith Block, Mary F. Holahan, Paulette Dunn Hennum, Margo Prentiss, Kittu Gates, Wendy McFarland Outland, Carol T. Larsen, Dan Wharton, Shraga Edelsbury, Margarita Laughlin, and Allyn Lord.

Early in the work, New York colleagues—David Hupert, Merle B. Gordon, M. J. Gladstone, Nancy McGary, David Epstein, and Lyda Moller—advised and encouraged.

Later from Washington an extended company counseled, cautioned, and conferred. My gratitude goes to Martha Morris Shannon, Katherine P. Spiess, Katherine M. Sprague, Barbara Belcher, Kathy A. Kuthz, Holman J. Swinney, Albina DeMeio, Alice Bryant, Louis Goldich, Richard Porter, John Buchannan, Barbara Redjinski, Michael S. Bell, Ted Greenberg, Renee Montgomery, and Deborah Cooper.

Each author persevered as the book evolved to its present voice and tone. I will treasure the dialogue and the ideas that each gave freely and that I took on behalf of this work. Ellen Myette contributed unflagging enthusiasm and resourceful guidance at every stage. The glossary was fashioned by Ann-Marie Reilly; and the registrar's book shelf was crafted by Dana Stein Dince and Martha Battle. Photographs were researched and organized by Lynn Berg and Deanna Kerrigan. The proofreading proceeded patiently in Melanie Dzwonchyk's able hands.

Ed Able said yes when we needed it the most. He and AAM staff —Kathy Dwyer, Jim Trulove, and Susan Waterman— propelled us into final action.

This book was produced, in part, through generous contributions from Huntington T. Block and Carol and H. Daniel McCollister who have given, as well, time and expertise to the museum community.

That the work proceeded at all is due to the daily support I receive at the museum from Tom Freudenheim, Freida Austin Hancock, Joe Wiley, and Jane Sledge and at home from Will Lowe.

Finally, more than any other person, Ligeia Fontaine shaped this book, brought harmony to the writing styles, encouraged and gently steered us to the printed page. She has become a trusted friend and valued advisor. I thank her for her thoughtful contributions, her humor, and her sensitive treatment of the people and ideas that make this book.

Mary Case, Editor

How This Book Came to Be

Washington, D.C., in June is a very appealing town, especially to the visitor. The temperature does not yet rival that of New Delhi, the Mall is green and inviting, and the city's many garden plots are still in flower. Furthermore, from the Sheraton Park Hotel, site of the 1976 annual meeting of the American Association of Museums (AAM), it is an easy walk to wonderful museums, historic mansions, and the federal monuments. Why then, after a full day's workshops and meetings, would forty-three registrars choose to remain indoors?

In a crowded hotel room, these registrars were in fact taking the first step of a professional journey. The immediate goal of this late afternoon conclave was to establish a registrars' steering committee, choose its officers, and determine its structure. Its most pressing long-term goal was to become a standing professional committee of the AAM. Both of these goals were means to an end; the underlying and most critical objective of the assembled registrars was to advance their profession.

In 1976, registrars' concerns were scarcely reflected in the annual meeting program, nor were registrars represented on the AAM council. The registrars were convinced that something had to be done to inform their museum colleagues of the changing role of the registrar and to promote communication among themselves. Thanks to the activities of the Registrars Committee and to the hard work of registrars all over the country, these aims have now become reality. *Registrars on Record* commemorates these efforts.

Introduction

The Book and its Uses

If *Museum Registration Methods*[1] is the technical bible of the profession, *Registrars on Record* is the book that bears sometimes wry witness to the experience of being a registrar. In a series of journalistic essays, thirteen very different people, some registrars and others not, reflect upon museum registration, focus on some of its special characteristics as a discipline, and speculate about its future. Some of the essayists talk about how they go about their work and give advice on how to proceed. Others look at the history and development of the profession. Still others examine the considerable impact of automation on the profession and discuss the possible consequences of the computer revolution on museum work.

Because *Registrars on Record* is not a "how to" book so much as a "getting acquainted" book, it should appeal to a broad audience. For example, the new museum director, who has spent a lifetime in astrophysics or fund raising, and lacks direct museum experience, can pick up this text for an introduction to some important aspects of the museum world. Ditto for the new administrator or trustee, whose expertise is often confined to business and finance. Though the lens through which the authors look is focused on museum registration, many of the fundamentals of museum work can be seen.

At the other end of the museum hierarchy, the docent, the volunteer, the student, and the intern will also find something here. The writers speak of the excitement and turmoil of putting together an exhibition, of the challenges of information management, of the attention to detail required by such tasks as collections inventory. To the person contemplating a career as a museum registrar, this book will convey something of the actual feel of daily work.

For those in the profession, or closer to it, the book offers a confirmatory experience or a jumping off point for dialogue. Many registrars will see themselves reflected in these pages; others will take exception to some of what is said, and this is as it should be. Collections managers, and individuals in related fields, will be interested to see the similarities, and sometimes the overlap, between their professions and that of the museum registrar. Subject matter specialists and conservators, with whom registrars so frequently work, will get a sharper sense of the challenges of coordinating between disciplines.

Though *Registrars on Record* is meant to commemorate the founding of the Registrars Committee, it does more than that. The book is a tribute to a dozen years of hard work by leaders and novices alike, a dozen years that have seen the maturation of both the committee and the profession. During this period many have done yeoman's labor and contributed to the development of an effective professional organization. The evolution of this organization warrants review.

A Brief History of the Registrars Committee

The founding members of the committee were dedicated to strengthening the profession and giving registrars a unified voice with which to address their colleagues in the museum world. They proposed a list of activities that they felt would improve communication between registrars and give structure and identity to the profession. The members wished to foster opportunities for registrars to meet and exchange ideas—notably at regional and annual meetings, where the committee planned to organize workshops and ad hoc sessions. The publication of materials of use to registrars was also strongly advocated. The first items on this agenda were a newsletter and a mailing list, followed by a position and salary survey, and a statement on professional practices.

Many of these goals were quickly realized. Barely three months after the Washington meeting, workshops by and for registrars were scheduled for all six of the AAM regional conferences. (These were the first of a long, impressive list of workshops and seminars sponsored by the increasingly active regional groups.) By May of the following year, the Registrars Committee became a standing professional committee of the AAM;

its bylaws, approved at the June meeting in Seattle, stated the committee's purposes:

This registrar's committee shall give assistance to AAM and to its regional conferences in their objectives of sound professional preparation and promotion of high standards, and specifically, shall endeavor to increase programs and publications, establish standards of professional practices, and create an atmosphere of understanding and respect, of communication and cooperation among registrars, between registrars and other museum professionals, and between registrars and individuals in related service fields.

Over the next decade, the Registrars Committee sought to put these ideals into practice. Through its subcommittees, task forces, and through the diligence of individual members who took on special assignments, the Registrars Committee engaged in numerous projects that contributed both to the profession and to the larger museum world.

The committee and its members worked in cooperation with many other groups and institutions. These have included the American Management Association, the Women's Caucus of the AAM, the Center for Advanced Study in Education at the City University of New York, Museums Collaborative, Inc., the Smithsonian's Museum Reference Center, the Archives of American Art, and the Association of Art Museum Directors. Projects varied widely, from the development of training materials to the writing of an insurance manual.

The specialized interests of registrars were addressed by subcommittees and task forces. Task force guidelines were developed to ensure that all projects sponsored by the committee would be pursued in a timely manner and would address the needs of the entire profession. Over the years, task forces explored such issues as condition reports, loan agreements, and synthetic packing materials. These task forces engaged in intensive research, prepared grant proposals when appropriate, and regularly reported their conclusions to the committee.

Other projects that aroused keen interest among members included the salary survey questionnaire, the development of future objectives—which provided members with a broad range of options for future activities—and the professional practices statement, submitted and ratified at the AAM's annual meeting in 1981. Another milestone was the code of ethics for registrars (see Appendix).

Communication among registrars was a committee concern from the very beginning. The committee encouraged its members to identify educational needs and, if possible, to respond to them. One of the most successful efforts by a committee member was *Registrars' Report*. (For several years, beginning in 1977, each issue of this report discussed a specialized topic, seeking to convey a basic level of understanding.) The committee advised its members to write, to circulate unpublished papers, and to submit material for publication to *Museum News*. The Registrars Directory, published in 1980, served as a national locator. Future editions came out in 1985 and 1987. An archives task force organized and centralized committee records; a publications task force was formed in the wake of the first issue of the committee's newsletter, *Registrar* (1984).

As the committee flourished, its influence grew. The committee increased communication with other professional standing committees of the AAM by formalizing mail exchange and by directing regional chairs to meet with their counterparts in other disciplines. Beginning in 1980, committee members became AAM councilors. The committee also sent representatives to consult with the Museum Assessment Program (MAP), and the Commission on Museums for a New Century. Members contributed to the development of *The Official Museum Products and Services Guide*.[2]

In the last three years, the committee has completed standards of practice for couriers (see Appendix), produced a standardized facilities report, and developed prototypes for formal internships and entry level professionals. In 1985 the committee presented an ambitious five-year plan to its members and to the AAM council. The plan included the biennial publication of the Registrars Directory, promoting workshops and sessions at regional, national, and international levels, and a generally higher level of involvement in international activities. The committee also looked forward to more research on such topics as facilities reports and criteria for personnel accreditation. Publishing *Registrars on Record* was another important goal.

What does the future hold for the Registrars Committee? As registrars become more involved in policy making, collections management, and the creation of information management systems, there will be a call for increased education. Formal training, workshops, and publications will have to answer this need. The committee will respond by helping to design museum studies curricula for registrars, by encouraging continuing education, and by promoting liaison with other museum professionals, especially conservators. Standards for transportation, shipping, and packing will have to be established, particularly in the face of a changing transportation industry. Professional standards for all levels will be refined, affirmative action is expected to remain a priority, and the emerging issue of personal safety in the work place is expected to get attention.

The Registrars Committee has been a strong, active arm of the AAM, constantly striving to meet the needs of its membership, the profession, and the wider museum community. The committee will meet the challenges of the next decade by continuing to foster a spirit of understanding, respect, and cooperation among registrars and other museum professionals.

Notes

[1] Dorothy H. Dudley, Irma Wilkinson, et al., *Museum Registration Methods* (Washington, D.C.: American Association of Museums) was originally published in 1958. Since that time, the text has been the basic technical reference for registrars. A revised third edition was published in 1979.

[2] *The Official Museum Products and Services Guide* (Illinois: National Register Publishing Company and the American Association of Museums, 1983).

The Role of
the Registrar

NAME	CHARACTER OF OBJECT	LOCALITY	RECEIVED FROM	COLLECTED BY		REMARKS

From Clay Tablet to Hard Disk

VIRGINIA MANN

The first time I ever went to a museum I was five years old. That was in the 1940s. My father took me to the Smithsonian. There were no Acoustiguides. No docents. There were hardly any people. My father and I whispered. I learned a lot that day, and going to museums became a treat that my father and I shared while I was growing up.

Today's museums do not depend solely on parents to explain what the exhibits are all about. This is the information age. Museums have assumed the educational role with every didactic and sensational teaching aid they can summon. Their audiences approve. All over the United States, more and more people are searching out the lessons that can only be taught by museums.

America's museums are still young, courageous, and sometimes awkward institutions. The first museum in the United States was founded in 1773 by the Library Society of South Carolina; by 1876, there were still only about two hundred museums in the United States.[1] Now, there are over six thousand, and they can be found in every region, and in almost every community. This boom includes museums of all sorts: art, natural history, science, technology, ethnography, history, botanical gardens, aquariums, and zoos. Nearly all of these museums are dedicated to delighting and edifying an ever-growing public.

As the Commission on Museums for a New Century notes, "Our nation's museums have a long tradition of scholarship, education, and public service. Their contributions to our intellectual and cultural life, their capacity for inquiry and vision, make them cornerstones of a democratic society."[2] Perhaps it is this democratic thrust of ours that makes our museums so popular. Or perhaps, to receive public support, museums must have broad appeal. Whatever the reason, museums are increasingly responsive to their audiences, increasingly visited, and increasingly accountable.

The museum as a public institution is a relatively modern phenomenon. Originally, museums were private. The most famous museum in the ancient world was founded by Ptolemy the First in Alexandria in 332 B.C. It collected books and artifacts, and information about them. It had a cataloguing system. "It was the world's first think tank."[3]

Public museums seem to have been a Roman invention. When in 189 B.C. the Roman general Fluvius returned from battle with a booty of bronze and marble statues and other treasures, he built a temple to display the hoard. This must have been one of the first times that objects synonymous with the wonder of the past were exhibited to the public.[4] But after the collapse of the Roman Empire, this innovation was forgotten for centuries. With the rise of Christianity, and the evolution of a feudal hierarchy, it became customary to collect treasures that would enhance the prestige of religion and of the social institutions dear to the nobility. These formed the basis for collections in Medieval Europe. The awakening of interest in classical material during the Renaissance gave rise to many fine collections, particularly in the Italian city states. These collections were private, shared only among the elite or with scholars patronized by the church, the nobility, or the wealthy.

It wasn't until the sixteenth and seventeenth centuries that the first public museums, intended as centers of research, were established. Many of these were associated with seats of learning; such were the University Museum in Basel, and the Ashmolean in Oxford. In the eighteenth century larger museums, like the British Museum and the Louvre, opened their doors. They were followed in the nineteenth century by national galleries and museums specifically dedicated to the citizen's use and pleasure.

All of these institutions had to have some way of keeping

track of their holdings. Thus it was that the rise of public museums went hand in hand with the development of systematic classification and cataloguing. From the very beginning, then, museums were not only collecting objects, but devising means of classifying these objects and organizing the information about them.

How did early systems of classification used by museums in the past evolve into the modern system? No one seems to know very much about this subject, and I have not been able to find a written history of museum registration. Nevertheless, the history of record keeping extends far back in time; the scribe who kept inventory lists of the royal household's goods on clay tablets was an ancestor of the registrar.

In the several thousand years between the clay tablet and the computer, there were many experiments in record keeping. Certainly, commerce and trade demanded sophisticated approaches to inventory control. New accounting methods were invented and clerks and bookkeepers proliferated. The museum registrar of the turn of the century was a cousin to the bookkeeper, a recorder who registered objects into the museum in a ledger book.

A typical ledger book entry (this one from 1913)[5] reads:

440262 Venetian Glass Vase:
    black ground, decorated with yellow and blue.
    Style "Vetro Fenecio,"
    received from M. Camerino, Venice, Italy, Apr. 22/13

In cases—and there are many—where no research has been done, something like this entry may still be the primary record for the object. This record will be kept by the registrar forever. Eventually, the record's image may be stored on hard disk, or laser disk, or whatever is yet to be invented.

This example illustrates some of the fundamental differences between the clerk and the registrar, differences that would have been as true a hundred years ago as they are today. The first is that while the bookkeeper usually tracks a more or less balanced flow of items in and items out, the registrar more often records "goods received." There is always more coming into the museum than leaving it; consequently, the registrar's records are always getting larger—and more unwieldy.

The second difference is that while the bookkeeper's records are principally important as a mirror of the traffic of goods, or flow of monies, the museum's records themselves have substantial intellectual status and are of inestimable value. The upkeep of these records, their accuracy and accessibility, are central to the museum's mission.

The basic purposes of a museum are to collect, preserve, exhibit, and interpret. "Museums collect," says Edward Alexander, "because they believe that objects are important and evocative survivals of human civilization worthy of careful study and with powerful educational impact. Museums thus carefully preserve their holdings so as to transmit important information to the present generation and posterity."[6] None of this can be done without the data maintained in the registration system.

The holdings of a museum include the objects, artifacts, and specimens in its collections. These holdings are rightly considered national treasures, and in fact are part of a nation's assets. It is the curator's job to give these assets a voice. When curators select objects for the collection, they give the collection shape and meaning. When they decide how to combine and re-combine a collection's parts into exhibitions, or when they analyze specimens for scientific study, they are making decisions about how to describe the history of the planet or of civilization.

Beside the curator stands a large supporting cast. Among the cast members is the registrar, who is both the collections manager and record keeper. For if the physical collections are the museum's first concern, its second are the records. Without records, objects and specimens are virtually meaningless.

Record keeping provides the basis for communicating information about the objects in the collection. Cataloguing and cross-referencing systems allow the collection to be viewed under differing classifications. Many people make use of these systems and this information—colleagues within the museum, outside researchers, the public at large. All benefit from a sophisticated approach to gathering and maintaining information.

But the registrar is much more than an information specialist. Indeed, the registrar oversees and controls all object movement, both within the museum and without, and is responsible for the surrounding functions of risk management, storage, packing, object handling, and inventory control. A registrar's knowledge must include art history or archaeology or science or history or technology; it must embrace insurance, taxes, shipping, packing techniques, customs, photography, fumigation, and computer science. A registrar must be conversant with such terms as ormolu, Kilim, Churinga, wall-to-wall, airway bill, cockling, foxing, polyurethane, pro-forma invoice, megabyte, I/O configuration, and relational database.

Like movie moguls who started with nickelodeons, the responsibilities of the registrar have grown exponentially; the job description now encompasses a myriad of complex duties. Within the museum, the registrar is the mogul of information management. What the registrar does with information, and how he or she does it, influences the uses to which the holdings are put by the curator or, in fact, anyone else.

Reality is based on perception. How museum collections were perceived a century ago, how they are perceived now, and how they will be perceived a century hence, all depend largely on the information gathered and preserved about those collections. The museum selects, edits, and defines information, mirroring the changing contextual concerns, and thereby shaping perceptions.

A century ago, the average person thought of a dolphin as a big scary fish, like a shark. Today a dolphin is a friendly mammal who can talk. The dolphin has been studied, both in the field and in museum and aquarium contexts; subsequent presentation and information management have changed our view of the dolphin. The same kind of changes have occurred in many fields: whether we speak of marine life, impressionist paintings, or Afro-American history, the presentation of information has altered attitudes. Facts may be collected endlessly, but it is their application that helps us understand the world.

There are different kinds of facts about collections, and the registration system holds a great many of them. For example, the registrar handles the legal information that establishes ownership, or the terms under which an object, or collection, is in the museum's custody. The registrar also monitors the information about the care and movement of objects. Finally, the registrar is responsible for identification and catalogue data. It is the identification data that are now undergoing radical change.

The columnar ledger page of the nineteenth century evolved into a multi-card system based on the Library of Congress catalogue with its author and subject indices. Initiated in 1906 by the Metropolitan Museum of Art in New York, most art museums adopted this system, or a variant, in the decades that followed.

How does this system work? First, a predetermined set of information about an object is recorded. In an art museum, for example, sets of cards are produced and cross-filed under such headings as accession number, artist or maker name, donor name, vendor name, functional type, ex-collection, and location. (Sometimes, other rubrics are added.) These headings are further subdivided geographically and chronologically; some museums subdivide by subject. Other cross-references may also exist, for example style, technique, or material. These cards are often arranged differently from museum to museum, depending on the nature of the collections or on the museum's traditional way of doing things.

This kind of cataloguing makes it possible to answer such questions as: Where is the Renoir painting *Woman in Pink?* How many Italian paintings are there in the collection? Do you have any pre-Columbian baskets? What did my grandfather, Elmo Peartree, give to the museum?

As demands for information increase, questions become more complex. The development officer wants a list of those donors who between 1980 and 1985 gave gifts valued at over five thousand dollars. A curator calls from another museum, inquiring about the number of inlaid Federal card tables in the furniture collection. A historian asks: "What nineteenth-century European paintings does the museum own that were previously in private American collections?" A visitor wants to know how many images of dogs there are in the collection. The attorney general wants to know how many objects are in the collection and what percentage are missing. The insurer wants to know the total estimated value of objects in storage.

Less and less easily is the registrar able to extract answers to such questions from the manual system. An incommodious mountain of data has accumulated; access is at best cumbersome. This is the point at which dreams of electronic sugarplums begin to dance in the heads of registrars; this is the point at which many museums take their registrar's advice and begin automating the registration system.

It is too soon to predict the precise effects of computerized registration systems on the museums of America. That automation will have effects is certain. Registration systems themselves will undergo successive refinement. New uses for information will arise. Things that none of us have yet thought of will be done using our new electronic allies. The character of exhibitions, of museum education, of relations with the public, will alter. Some changes will be subtle, others revolutionary.

It's a long way from the clay tablet, or even the ledger, to the hard disk. But from a broad historical perspective, the evolution from clerk to information manager is just the beginning. The next few decades will bring profound change to the profession, including increased responsibility and probably requiring increased expertise and education. The information age is a new era for everyone, but especially for those who manage data every day. This is an exciting time to be a registrar.

Notes

[1] G. Ellis Burcaw, *Introduction to Museum Work* (Nashville: American Association for State and Local History, 1975), 26.

[2] *Museums For A New Century* (Washington, D.C.: American Association of Museums, 1984), 17.

9

[3]Lional Casson, "Triumphs from the Ancient World's First Think Tank," *Smithsonian* Vol. 16, No. 3 (June 1985): 159.

[4]Dillon Ripley, *The Sacred Grove* (New York: Simon and Shuster, 1969), 25.

[5]From a ledger of the Golden Gate Museum, now part of the Fine Arts Museums of San Francisco.

[6]Edward P. Alexander, *Museums in Motion: An Introduction to the History of Functions of Museums* (Nashville: American Association for State and Local History, 1979), 119.

What Registrars Do All Day

MARY CASE

At a fund-raising dinner, I exchange names with the tuxedoed gentleman on my right who then asks me what I do for a living. When I tell him I am the museum's registrar his face reflects interest—quickly followed by polite confusion. He then presses me for an explanation.

In this situation I usually say, "I keep track of the stuff in the museum's collection," and hope that the conversation can go on to other topics. But instead of dropping the subject, the gentleman says: "I go to museums, of course, but I never realized that anyone had to keep track of the collection. Makes sense, though. But tell me, what is it exactly that you keep track of? The stuff that's on display? Or does it include what you store?"

These are naive questions, but not dumb ones. Even museum aficionados imagine museums as having only two parts: the exhibition areas and storage, a locale of mythical proportions where forgotten treasures await rediscovery. If reminded of laboratories, libraries, and even loading docks, the museumgoer will of course acknowledge that these must exist, but they are not what the word "museum" evokes. In part, this is because the museum community itself habitually emphasizes its most valuable, most beautiful, most fashionable, and rarest objects, but seldom tells the public about how museums work.

No wonder, then, that the dinner guest is uninformed. Even museum professionals sometimes stumble in their attempts to describe what a registrar does. Nor is this surprising. The registrar's role has undergone considerable change over the past decade; and the position is still evolving.

To explain my job I begin by describing museum collections.

The Role of the Registrar

I tell my new acquaintance that collection items can reside almost anywhere in the museum—exhibit areas, storerooms, labs, someone's desk drawer, a file cabinet, a card catalogue, or even a computer disk. Collections, I emphasize, are comprised not only of objects or specimens, but of documents and data. The objects and specimens, known as the physical collection, increase in historic, scientific, and economic value when supported by documents and data, known as the intellectual collection.

"What kind of documents?" he wants to know. "Many different kinds," I answer. "There are official and legal transaction forms such as deeds of gift, bills of sale, loan contracts, and accession and acquisition records. There are donor and artist biographies, correspondence, field notes, scientific analyses, business archives, manuscripts, and published materials. The documentation record even includes photos and negatives, film, audio and video records."

The physical collection (I continue) is only useful to the museum when it is accompanied by information. Some objects, like a Renaissance portrait or a reconstructed dinosaur skeleton, are so aesthetically pleasing or so dramatic that they communicate directly to the museum visitor; but even these objects increase in interest if we know that the first is the Mona Lisa and the second a tyranosaurus rex. The more we know, the more interesting and valuable they become.

Attaching appropriate information to objects and specimens is what museum professionals call interpretation. And museums are really in the interpretation business. Their true end product is the knowledge, sometimes even the wisdom, expressed in an exhibition, or found in a scholarly journal, a catalogue, an educational program, a public lecture—anything that advances human understanding. That can only be done if both the physical and intellectual collections are readily available.

"Is that where you come in?" asks my neighbor. "That's right. I make sure that everything is in its proper place. I do that by overseeing the operations that affect collections and by managing risk, space, information, and people."

What Registrars Do All Day

Sometimes an interlocutor is not just making conversation but is genuinely interested in finding out more. That is the case with this man. Bluntly, he says: "I know how risk, space, information, and people are managed—or mismanaged—in my own business. But I don't have the slightest idea how those things are done in a museum. If that's the job of a museum registrar, what do you actually do? How do you spend your day?"

The specificity of his question arouses my suspicions; I ask if by any chance he isn't a newly elected trustee? "As a matter of fact," he smiles, "I am. As you can tell," he adds, putting on the charm, "I know nothing about museums. I am counting on you to begin my education." "Alright," I say, taking him at his word, "I'll tell you what I did today."

Just A Routine Twenty-Hour Day

Today began early, at 3:00 a.m., when I rose to meet a customs broker. We drove to the designated hangar at the international airport. There we met the courier, the security officials, and the packers. We quietly loaded an unmarked truck with forty-three million dollars worth of art and delivered it to the museum's secure storage in the suburbs. By now it's 6:00 a.m.—time for coffee and a bagel.

After the break, I drove back to the city in the van with the driver and an art handler. We went to pick up a painting, a Boudin, from a private lender. When we got the painting down, the lender suddenly developed second thoughts. That bare spot on the wall is often disquieting. I tried to reassure her and told her that the handling, insurance, and security would all be impeccable.

Back at the museum I checked that the three volunteers— graduate students in art history—were indeed cataloguing the group of recently accessioned Steinlen posters. I gave a call downstairs to the inventory clerk. His sleuthing paid off: he found the Gallé vase (missing from its shelf in storage) in the conservation lab. Somehow, the right paperwork never got

15

filed. Then on to the cafeteria for lunch with the curator of decorative arts; over the yogurt, I gave her an impromptu tutorial on the computerized collections management system that we are installing.

At two o'clock I showed up at the director's office for a meeting. The subject was a proposed change to the collections management policy; by three, we had hammered out a draft to be distributed to the staff. Back in my office, I found two bids from transport companies in my "In Box." (Less than a year from now, we'll be sending our Impressionists—valued at more than fifty million dollars—to Chicago, New Orleans, and San Francisco.) I reviewed the bids, and then squeezed in a call to another registrar with whom I'm leading a workshop at the next professional meeting. I was still on the phone when my staff photographer arrived for his performance appraisal. The appraisal took only twenty minutes, but he and I also had to discuss completing the photo documentation of some items that are scheduled to go out on loan.

When I was finally ready to leave the office a phone call came through from an architect; he's with the firm that will build the museum's new wing. Construction is to begin two years from now; we're in the planning phase. He'd received my recommendations for storage design and wanted to set up a meeting. I stalled, telling him that the security chief, who should attend our meeting, can't make it till the end of next week. Halfway out the door I suddenly remembered that I absolutely had to call the general counsel's office about that donated Corot. I've got misgivings about the transaction, and I'd rather be thought persnickety than be sued by the French government. But I have to admit that the biggest question for me was not the possibility of an international scandal but whether I could keep my eyes open during tonight's dinner.

"Is that all?" says the new trustee. "No, it's not." I decide to take the chance and explain as much as I can before the end of the sumptuous meal. I have six courses during which to tell him about my work. This is what I say:

What a Registrar Does

If we break down the registrar's work day into tasks we can see that the registrar does indeed manage space, risk, information, and people, and that the number of things to do is immense. But if we were to follow the registrar for a week, or even a month, the responsibilities would keep multiplying. At some time during that month the registrar, helped by the registration and other museum staff, might do the following:

- make entries to the records
- conduct inventories of the collections
- accession and deaccession objects or specimens
- evaluate the condition of objects or specimens
- photograph objects or specimens
- give basic care to objects
- catalogue museum objects
- answer questions from colleagues or members of the public about specific objects or specimens
- negotiate contracts with movers, insurance agencies, and transportation companies
- formulate the logistics of international or domestic traveling exhibitions
- supervise packing and unpacking of traveling exhibitions
- accompany, as a courier, the objects and specimens as they travel
- train staff and volunteers
- manage personnel
- devise an information system, or, develop a computerized records management system
- establish work schedules
- establish security standards
- coordinate an exhibition

- develop policies and procedures
- help plan facilities
- determine budgets

Is all this demanded of every registrar? It depends. The size and type of museum, the history of growth within the institution, and the credentials and abilities of the individual registrar and of the registration unit are all factors that influence the registrar's duties.

In a large museum, a registrar will have greater administrative responsibility and will necessarily spend more time on personnel management, budgets, and scheduling. Because large museums tend to engage attorneys, risk managers, conservators, and other specialists, the registrar will frequently meet and discuss emergent issues with these colleagues. But in a small museum, where duties collapse into fewer employment positions, a registrar may wear many hats. In either case, the registrar must have proficiency with the principles of museology.

Why the Registrar Does It

To what purpose all this activity? What is the unifying theme? As a compendium of tasks, the whole does not really hang together. But an examination of the registrar's original role, the keeping of the museum's records, provides some clues.

In the past, the museum registrar simply wrote down what entered the collection and what left it. Supervised by the curator or scientist, the registrar's flourishes of practiced penmanship appeared in a large, columned book called the register. Therein were recorded the place and date of collection; the type and description of the specimen; its cost or value; the name and address of the donor, vendor, or collector. Only at the behest of his or her superior would the registrar add further detail.

Today's registrar is no longer supervised by the curator, doesn't write in ink, may never have seen a register, but is still responsible for keeping the museum's records. This central duty remains at the core of the profession, and is the anchor for the registrar's other tasks.

How can this be? The records of today bear little resemblance to those of yesterday. For one thing, there is more information: not only are collections larger, but more data are recorded about individual objects. Also, information is more valued; considered part of the collection, it is the foundation of knowledge upon which the museum rests. Finally, there is a greater demand for information. Museums need information to fulfill their ethical and legal obligations; scholars and scientists need information to do their work; and officials representing the interests of the public ask astute questions about how museums safeguard their collections, dispose of objects, and spend money.

For all of these reasons, the registrar's record keeping function has expanded and new recording methods, supported by new technologies, have developed. The registrar no longer simply records information but manages it, making sure that the right people get the right information at the right time.

Nevertheless, current record keeping activities enjoy significant parallels with those of the past. Records have been kept, and are still kept, for two primary reasons: to make collection items accessible and to account for them. When accurate data exist it is easier to locate and identify an object, easier to study it, preserve it, care for it, exhibit it. When accurate data exist, an object is harder to steal, fake, or lose. If the object is stolen, or lost, or damaged, accurate data will make it easier to recover or repair. Information about an object is a kind of survival mechanism for the object, but it is a mechanism that only we can provide.

From record keeping and its basic purposes spring the twin themes of the registrar's working life, access and accountability.

Museum professionals use the term *access* to indicate that museums not only permit but encourage the use of collections; *accountability* means that museums accept responsibility for the care and control of the collections. Everything the registrar does aims at one or both of these targets. Everything the registrar does translates into a conflicting goal: protect the collection and make it available to colleagues and to the public. As one registrar put it: "Museums put everything into a box and then lock it. Then they give everyone the key."

It is in the nature of museums to have two kinds of people working with the collections. At one extreme are those who would prefer to preserve collections in lightless rooms disturbed only by the mechanical hum of air purifying equipment and attended day and night by armed guards. At the other extreme are equally well-meaning enthusiasts who want the museum's most fragile ewer (or rarest fossil) to be on perpetual exhibit, and/or easily available to visiting scholars and school children.

Registrars serve museums by assessing potential risks to collections. When, for example, a museum is about to launch itself into a building program, it is likely to be the registrar who suggests several smaller rather then a single large storage room. This, the registrar will insist, could reduce traffic, allow for more specifically controlled environments, or avoid a catastrophic loss. But the registrar will also make just as detailed recommendations to give the public more immediate access to collections.

Ethics

In every museum, someone has to balance accountability against access; someone has to keep both of these fundamental priorities in mind. Officially, this is the director's job; as a practical matter, it falls to the registrar.

At its core, then, the registrar's role is essentially ethical, and like most vocations based on ethics, its expression in daily work is beset by difficulties. The registrar espouses the ethical principle that a museum must satisfy a public trust, and that this trust implies exhibitions, research, public programs, as well as the preservation, even the nurturing, of each object, artifact, and specimen. The lowliest annelid worm in a natural science museum must be coddled; to someone, it is precious, and for all we know, may hold the key to a scientific mystery.

Thus the registrar assumes the role of protector of the collections in the face of potential threats to physical safety and intellectual disorder. But threats to the collections include the normal business activities of a museum.

Collections, for example, may be damaged by exposure to exhibition light. Movement and handling, even in the relative safety of the museum, expose fragile canvases and delicate decorative arts to risk. Rare zoo animals are lent internationally to widen gene pools but travel is stressful to the animal, as is adjustment to the new environment. Research can destroy an object. Doing nothing—allowing the collections to sit unattended in storage—brings other risks. Dirt accumulates, insects are attracted, objects age, chemicals evaporate, varnish darkens, wooden joints loosen, textiles split, iron rusts. Worse, intellectual confusion arises when the information that fixes provenance and attribution becomes disassociated from the object.

Deciding between the sometimes conflicting mandates (access versus accountability) or simply adhering to either of those mandates creates tensions in the registrar's work life that reveal themselves in a thousand ways. Yes, the panel paintings are central to the folk art exhibition that is traveling to rural communities depicted in the works, but will they survive the environmental fluctuations? How will the pandas fare on the long trip from Beijing; will they thrive in the local climate? Should the museum accept the donation of an interesting and valuable collection of mollusks when its own collection has never been examined by researchers and, if truth be told, is not either properly documented or fully accessioned?

Many ethical problems faced by the registrar spring from restricted resources, for example: the museum can no longer support off-site storage. Collections are scheduled to move to a sub-basement of the old courthouse. Security there is lax, the place is damp and dirty, and there is no time to pack anything carefully. Or: The staff is overloaded. The cyclical inventory of antique weapons has slipped behind schedule, which imperils the museum's insurance coverage. But fixing the skylight in the costume hall has left construction dust that may, no, *will,* harm the textiles. The museum collection is fundamental to museum programs but care of the collection is a constant drain on scarce staff time and institutional finances. Every museum in America struggles to balance the rising cost of collections care against research and interpretation. Where resources are limited, choices are often made that are morally troubling. The question "Is it worth doing?" refers not just to the intellectual value of an exhibition but the resources it will absorb.

Another arena where ethics come into play are the museum's legal affairs. Potential legal problems in a registrar's office are the same as those encountered by almost any business operation except, of course, that the body of legislation differs significantly. When a museum encounters theft, fraud, or embezzlement what is at stake is not private property or corporate funds but a public trust.

Who says "no" to the donor who wants to backdate the donation to a more advantageous tax year? What is the registrar's responsibility if the curator proposes to use museum collections for purposes other than those specified by the trust? Were the lizards or ivory or feathers or pre-Columbian art and artifacts imported in accordance with international regulations? Who retains what sort of copyright on the new contemporary piece purchased with restricted funds?

The registrar is the primary staff advisor to the director on such collection-related legal concerns. Not a lawyer, certainly, but a loyal and knowledgeable staff member who can, in confidence, suggest that the time to call legal counsel has arrived.

Ethical problems are normal to museum work. Were museum collections less vulnerable, and less valuable, many such problems would not exist. But museum administrators are in the peculiar position of managing a commodity that is at once a resource and a liability. Consequently, the dilemmas are endemic. They require constant analysis by the registrar—not just an assessment of the situation and possible solutions, but an examination of the values embodied by the proposed solution. Does the solution best advance the twin goals of access and accountability? Does it express the museum's mission and its responsibility to the public?

Working in a museum entails picking one's way through a mine field of ethical imbalances.

How does the administrator of a historic house weigh the role of the house as a coalescing element in the community against the protective, arms-length mandates of the museum profession? What options are open to the young museum studies graduate who discovers in the first month of employment that the collection of silver bowls and crystal vases are routinely commandeered by the powerful women's committee for its flower arranging classes? (The classes are given in the commodious living rooms of the town's wealthiest citizens: no special precautions are taken, no written records are made.) What does a curator do—other than storm and rage—when told a collection proposed for donation cannot be acquired because storage facilities are unavailable? In all of these situations, the registrar has a role.

Generally, when faced with resource scarcity, the registrar will argue for safety first—on the grounds that no interpretation can occur without a collection, and that the security of the collection is the preeminent legal obligation as well as the dominant ethical principle. Nevertheless, as we can see, this principle by no means resolves all predicaments.

Collections Management Policy

One way to reduce the number and severity of legal problems and ethical dilemmas is to have a strong collections management policy. The collections management policy is the governing tool used by museum administrators to regulate the development, use, and disposition of museum collections. It is frequently the registrar—who often encounters collegial frustration or wrath—

who agitates for a new and better policy. Furthermore, though management normally initiates policy making (and wise management solicits staff and board cooperation), it is the registrar who is most likely to be the policy's primary author and project manager.

The first and most important section of the collections management policy is a clear statement of the museum's overarching purpose, followed by specific goals. This statement must be broad enough to allow for growth and structured enough to guide and even limit the activities of a largely autonomous staff.

The policy regulates every activity surrounding collections development, standards of care and use, and disposition. Who will collect what? Who has authority to spend how much money and who will disburse funds from what accounts? Must adequate storage be identified before new collections are accepted? What constitutes adequate storage? Who has the authority to move objects? Who records the move? How will information be recorded and by whom? Who has authority over the content of the information? Over the format?

The collections management policy team will dissect each aspect of collection activity. In the process they will confront the deficiencies of their museum—backlogs, confused lines of authority, lack of adequate training, and always, not enough money. Policy making helps clarify values and goals, and gives a stamp of approval to certain compromises, and makes clear that others are not acceptable.

Colleagues and Consensus

To formulate policy and procedures is actually to play a co-ordinating role vis-à-vis collection activities. To do this, the registrar examines the disciplines covered by the museum—ethnography or art history or ichthyology—and identifies the standards of care suited to that discipline; from those standards, the registrar wrests the policies and procedures that will permit the museum and its staff to make the collection both safe *and* accessible.

This cannot be done without the help of museum colleagues.

They are the specialists who know about the intricacies of the collections. The registrar is the generalist, who must put all this information together into a coherent and acceptable form. Registrars deliberately work with others because successful collections management requires cooperative effort, and the policy directives must be based on consensus.

The registrar communicates regularly with the rest of the museum family, and tries to base the registration system on their needs. Conservators and preparators, transportation and insurance specialists, mount makers and photographers, information scientists and art handlers, all participate in collections management, as do museum directors, curators, designers, and trustees.

The registrar's network is inclusive. As a result, policy and procedures reflect a mix of opinions and serve many people, both inside and outside the museum. Furthermore, registrars are expected to operate equally well on the loading dock and in the board room. Far from being a profession that promotes isolation—the image is that of the registrar in a green eye shade, pouring over ledger books—museum registration requires a finely tuned ability to work with people.

The Registration Staff

Nowhere is this skill more useful than when dealing with registration staff. A registrar in a supervisory position depends on the goodwill, energy, and intelligence of the staff. Gaining the goodwill, and marshalling the intelligence and energy, are part of the registrar's job. But who is this personnel that the registrar must manage? The registrar usually supervises a mix of academically educated and technically trained personnel, as well as volunteers. In a typical registration unit, women outnumber men; indeed, eighty percent of registrars are women. Characteristically, the staff have more than a passing interest in the type of material preserved in the museum.

Registration staff are well educated. In an art museum, the staff usually have earned Masters of Arts degrees in art history; history and science museum registrars often have masters degrees in the humanities or sciences. Also appearing on resumes are masters degrees in business administration and in museum studies. The photographer on staff may hold a masters in fine arts. Information specialists may be graduates of the plethora of excellent university programs teaching information sciences. Collection specialists in the sciences often have their sights set on a Ph.D. Art or object handlers and preparators are often highly skilled craftspeople or artists with formal training or academic credentials. Secretaries, file clerks, and data entry specialists complete the registrar's contingent. Staff are frequently qualified beyond their current job status by education and experience and look forward to a rise in rank.

Because the duties assigned to the registrar are labor intensive and deadline driven, the registration staff is often the largest unit in the museum. In a historic house, for example, with a paid staff of seven, the registrar might supervise a clerk-typist, a collections manager who doubles as packer and photographer, and a dozen volunteers. Trained volunteers can catalogue, organize and number objects, conduct inventories, and give objects such basic care as dusting or repacking.

In a major art museum, the registrar may supervise an associate registrar for policy and special projects as well as three assistants, one assigned to permanent collections, one to handle in-house exhibitions and loans, another to manage traveling exhibitions. A team of art handlers, preparators, a photographer, and mount and crate makers move and hang and shoot the art. Cataloguing and inventory specialists, a computer manager, and data entry clerks and secretaries complete the staff. In a history museum, the staff inclines towards information management and inventory, care of collections in storage, public inquiry service, and interdepartmental coordination.

Employees recognize that efficiency is the hallmark of the registration unit and so they often suggest changes to enhance or simplify the system while increasing its usefulness. Such proposals should be seriously considered, and adopted whenever possible. Registration staff also adhere meticulously to approved procedures; they know that deviation produces blanks in the documentation and promotes careless handling of objects.

The staff of a registration unit are likely to have a passionate interest in their work. People are attracted to museum registration because they believe that the work contributes to society and also allows a high level of autonomy. Because registration is a team effort, it is suited to those whose personal satisfaction derives from a sense of shared values.

One of the typifying features of registrars (or of those who work in a registration unit) is that they are not bound to the office. They are just as likely to be at Storage Facility B as at their desk, or possibly they are with the curator in the exhibition area (or on a flight to New Guinea), or downstairs talking to the conservator in the lab, or entering data at the computer, or supervising an incoming shipment at the loading dock. If we take a closer look at the tasks performed in these areas, we can see that registrars continually encounter potential disorder, which they hold in check by strict allegiance to procedure.

Collections Processing

The museum equivalent of a pyramid's midpoint, the loading dock is the organization's focused energy center; it is where collections processing begins. Lumber, food, hazardous chemicals, mail, museum shop inventory, and collections material (much of it priceless and fragile) arrive through this portal. Despite the best scheduling efforts, they often arrive at the same moment.

This gives rise to disgruntled truck drivers, nervous security staff, bewildered custodial crews, and bickering department heads. A firm understanding of priorities—collections, spoilables, hazards—helps resolve such a situation, as do continuing efforts to stagger scheduled arrivals. The registrar's goal is to move collections efficiently and inconspicuously from the point of entry to a secure holding area.

Storage areas are among a registrar's favorite haunts. In museums, these take many forms. An object holding area is usually located near the loading dock and allows incoming material to be isolated in a controlled environment. Possible insect infestation is one reason to isolate new material. Protecting the materials is another. Organic materials react physically to new environments—changes in temperature and humidity can cause expansion and contraction. Incoming materials need time to acclimatize to the new surroundings.

One way museums meet the duel mandate of access and accountability is the "open" or study-storage area. These areas are open to the public and provide immediate access to the contents. Usually, physical collections are minimally identified on shelves or racks, or in drawers behind glass; collection information is available nearby from catalogue cards or by computer retrieval. Published material might also be available. The registrar is likely to be responsible for updating card files and computer entries, for daily reviews of the physical collection (or setting up such procedures with the security office), for removing and returning objects when necessary, and for answering inquiries from the public about the collection.

Closed storage is far more typical in a museum setting. Here, behind locked doors in darkened rooms, closets, garrets, vaults, bunkers, and basements, rest the nation's collective treasures. Planning for, organizing, and maintaining such facilities is a major collections management activity of museum registrars. Principles of internal control require the museum to institute and maintain procedures that prevent someone from removing both a physical specimen *and* its records from the collection. Storage planning must accommodate this requirement.

Yet another reason for the registrar's presence in storage is physical control of the collections. Retaining physical control over museum collections is an enormous task. At all times, museum administrators should be able to answer the questions "Where is it?" and "Who had it last?" Monitoring objects as they move around, or even out of, the museum is tedious but it is fundamental to security. In most museums, the collections management policy delegates the authority to track objects to the registrar, who performs regular inventories.

Exhibition Coordination

Registrars are problem solvers. Exhibitions are the perfect arena to demonstrate that skill because the overriding goal is to compel people to see in a new way. The extraordinary, the phenomenal, the rarest, the most, the largest, are all exhibition components. Budgets are never large enough, information is incomplete, plans change until opening night, and everyone needs something important done by the registrar NOW.

Because each exhibition intends to show something in a different way, no one on the exhibition team ever says, "Well, we'll do this one just like the one last fall." Instead everyone agrees that the fall show was good but that this one should be even better.

As with all museum activity, the director approves the exhibition concept, usually with the advice of an exhibition council composed of staff, board, and community members. The exhibition team is led by the content specialists—the curator or scientist or historian—and includes the designer, educator, registrar, conservator, and financial manager.

The registrar insures that the objects move safely and legally, arranges for crating and shipping, identifies and reduces risk potential, purchases insurance or arranges indemnification, records condition changes during the move and while on exhibition, and disperses the material at the end of the exhibition. If the exhibition travels, it may fall to the registrar to ensure that the exhibition team at each venue handles the materials properly, and that each new gallery is secure.

Because registrars are familiar with collection records, they are in a position to advise the exhibition team on object selection. For instance, the exhibition script calls for a mid-nineteenth century table setting. The curator is not quite sure which to choose. The registrar checks the records and discovers that of thirty-two tableware sets, only five have complete provenances. One set, once owned by President Lincoln, is too highly valued to fall within the insurance budget. One set was donated with the restriction that it be exhibited with a picture of the donor, thereby making it unusable in this exhibition context. The remaining three are strong possibilities.

Exhibition work is appealing because there is a beginning, a middle, and an end. There is focus and clarity and an opportunity for excellence. Excitement prevails, people stretch and strengthen their skills, camaraderie develops.

Documentation

Not all of the registrar's work is on this elevated plane. For example, the registrar must remember to budget for the enormously expensive acid-free paper stock for the museum's loan contracts and deeds of gift. On this paper, the registrar knows, will rest in perpetuity the record of a public trust. Endless stacks of precisely labeled file folders will be carefully filled with documents intended to protect legal standing, reveal provenance, and capture the many bits of information required to unlock the past and fix the place of every object in the collection.

Doing this work is akin to building a bridge for traffic that gets progressively heavier. Inevitably, dangerous potholes appear, the bridge begins to sag; it is time for resurfacing and buttressing. Repairs bog down traffic, but eventually the bridge reopens and the morning traffic report sings praise. Traffic resumes, increases, and the cycle begins anew.

Historically, documentation is the weakest link in collections care. In recent years, increased opportunities to share methods and techniques have resulted in improved documentation. In the near future, computerized systems are expected to bring greater refinement and maturity to this facet of museology.

Information Management

Registrars everywhere are lobbying more and more vociferously for their museums to invest in automated systems. Automation will improve access to collections information and strengthen security. Automation is also expected to reduce the tedium associated with endless detail work. In addition, registrars see information from a central vantage point. To a registrar, the similarities between specialties are apparent. The opportunity to pose broad questions about museum collections and to make connections between disciplines are among the other promises of technological advance.

Automated technologies include office automation systems, image processing systems, and systems to capture, store, and retrieve the enormous body of information about collections. Collections data range from physical description to provenance to associated people and events to bibliography and administrative details.

Although the automation of collections information has proceeded slowly over the past twenty years, it is now a matter of when, not if, museums will automate collections activities. Registrars lead the way in a natural progression from document specialists to information specialists.

Training

Registrars, hired for their qualifications, experience, and commitment to the work, usually train staff from all museum departments. Because museum directors recognize the central role of the registrar's office, new employees are frequently invited to intern with the registrar.

Training begins with the philosophical issues underlying collections accountability and access, many of which are sensitive and controversial. Who properly has access to collections? And when? Who owns research results? (Methods of capturing and retrieving information affect research efforts and can promote or impede useful research.) Who decides how to expend resources? Who is responsible for what forms of documentation?

Registrars stress that systems that store research data should link up with systems that manage the collections. The entomologist preparing to study morphos will be interested to learn that twenty-seven percent of the South American butterflies are about to leave the museum on loan. Knowing that the big Frankenthaler in the American collection is slated for conservation, or that the presidential china collection lacks three pieces to complete the set, or that there has been a marked increase in the number of inquiries about Indian skeletal remains are useful pieces of information for the collections manager who is attempting to use limited resources wisely.

Training sessions concentrate on ways to gain access to collections and on how to record the many details that enrich interpretation. Training extends to the specifics of documentation procedures, techniques of artifact handling and numbering, methods of photography, risk reductions, packing, and the preparation of condition reports and damage and loss reports.

What is a Registrar?

Registration was once hardship duty. As a fresh young college graduate, I was told that employment as a registrar would begin my preparation for curatorial work. The implication was that hard labor in the file room, on the loading dock, in the storage areas and freight elevator, was a prescribed rite of passage to the more exalted realm of curatorship.

This is no longer the case. Registrars have attained an identity of their own. They have their own variegated professional sphere. But there is always a dynamic tension in the registrar's work.

Not only is there the tension between the sometimes conflicting goals of access and accountability, but there are stylistic tensions built into the work itself. On the one hand, registrars are required to espouse the broadest possible view of museum collections—this enables them to formulate policy and procedures—and at the same time keep the narrowest possible perspective on the same collections—which enables them to pay attention to every necessary detail of documentation or information. Moreover, registrars are frequently in the position of reluctant revolutionaries. They value the traditions embodied in collections management systems yet are the apostles of change, always demanding that the systems be somehow bettered. Finally, registrars gather their rewards from a system that is at once stable and flexible, and from collections that are safe from damage and loss yet available for research and interpretation.

Perhaps it is these contradictions that make it so difficult to describe the registrar. Even within the profession itself, recent discussion of new titles—titles that would express the expanded nature of the registrar's work—illustrate the dilemma. Are registrars administrators or curators or directors for collections or collections management? Are they curators of documentation, exhibition coordinators, or collections information managers? Even many who value tradition may be dissuaded from retaining the title registrar because of its association with the original record keeping function—viewed as lacking interest and influence. As the profession evolves further the question of self-definition will be less of an issue, but the work will get better and richer and even more rewarding.

"I think," says the gentleman "that you have done me a great service—you've given me a window into a world few know exists, a world of complexity and paradox, of rigid patterns balanced by thoughtful care, of order and chaos—a kind of grand unified theory for museum work." To my utter amazement he continues, "And what do you plan to do tomorrow?"

The Registrar as Human Resource Manager

DANIEL B REIBEL

Every activity that goes on in today's museum involves not only objects but people. Conservators and curators, trustees and museum administrators, scientists and scholars, and the general public are among those who want frequent access to collections and to collections information.

All the people who interact with the museum's collections have their own special needs and demands. To accommodate these demands, museums develop policies and procedures. This web of policies, procedures, and people constitutes museum practice. Registrars are the guardians of this practice.

In a well-run museum it is impossible to acquire an object, store, exhibit, conserve, lend, or deaccession it without calling upon the registrar. Consequently, one of the registrar's principle tasks is to facilitate the interaction of people with the museum collection. Concurrently with managing data and physical collections, the registrar manages human resources.

Information, or data, are grist for the registrar's work. But information does not create itself nor does it access the collections—people do. Hence the essence of the registrar's task is to create, use, and audit systems that improve communication between people. The success or failure of the registration system is measured by how well people can use it. The sole purpose of the system is to preserve information about the museum collection to allow people to use the information and the objects themselves. The world's best data storage system is a failure if the information is inaccessible or if the rules of use are so arcane that only an anointed few understand them.

The Role of the Registrar

Museum policy controls human behavior. It fixes who can borrow or lend objects, and when and how and what the museum can accession or deaccession. It determines who has access to what information or to which objects.

The registration system embodies the collections management policy of the museum. The registrar develops and carries out procedures that derive from, and give substance to, policy mandates.

History

In the past, museum staff looked upon the registration system as an internal mechanism that accounted for collections. It was regarded as something akin to the payroll system, and it was expected to function about as invisibly. Registrars played an essential but scarcely a prominent role in the museum. Even where registrars were considered part of the professional staff, they enjoyed neither the status nor the rewards of, say, curators. Administrators had little interest in the registration system and paid scant attention to its function.[1]

These attitudes changed, for good reason. In the early 1970s, when the museum profession in the United States developed the concept of accreditation, the care of the collections became one of the primary characteristics of an accreditable museum. Essential to collections care are effective methods of record keeping and the ability to account for the collections responsibly. Museums that had never thought about registration, or had given it a low priority, suddenly discovered that a sound registration system was essential to museum practice. This principle was reinforced when one-fifth of the museums applying for accreditation failed to receive it because their collections care was inadequate. Museums that had been operating for years realized that they could not meet the minimum standards of accreditation because they had neglected a fundamental activity.

At the same time, trustees became increasingly alert to the responsibilities of stewardship. In addition to the usual problems of money, trustees began to face such emerging policy issues as race relations, labor relations, and the role of women. Highest on the list of changing concerns was collections accountability.

Cultural organizations suddenly found themselves held accountable by the public. Museums discovered that they could no longer acquire any object they pleased. Nor could they care for objects in any random fashion, or exhibit them or not, at whim. They could not discard objects without good reasons.

Museum boards came to acknowledge accountability not just for financial affairs but for collections activities. This new emphasis on accountability and collections care changed the role of the curator and expanded the roles of the registrar and the conservator. Museums that enjoyed neither the services of a registrar nor a conservator suddenly employed whole departments devoted to accounting for and caring for collections.

Furthermore, boards started developing policies that fit the new reality. Among these were broad collections management policies that addressed practical matters. What would the museum collect? How would it account for its collections? How would objects be deaccessioned? Who had authority to accession or deaccession? Although collections management policies were not new, suddenly every museum had to have one. An awareness of the importance of collections management had spread to the board room.

Policies and Policy Making

Although collections management policies appear to deal with physical things they actually govern human activities. They direct the behavior of the collective "we" that makes up the museum; they clarify the responsibilities of museum staff; they set boundaries. The policies declare that the museum will acquire only certain kinds of objects or specimens, that the director can spend up to a certain amount without board approval, that the conservator will conserve, and the registrar account for, collections.

A well-written policy incorporates the opinions of the board, the staff, and the public. The contribution of the professional staff to policy development varies from museum to museum. If the board is wise, it will set broad parameters and invite staff to develop the specifics. The best policies reflect the considerable experience of the professional staff.

Sometimes the board drafts the basic collections management policy and seeks comment from the staff. Often, staff tend to view the draft policy as a *fait accompli*. They write long, futile memoranda attacking the policy or decide that it could have been worse and accept the policy with misgivings. Neither of these tactics supports prudent museum practice.

Accepting an inadequate or unrealistic policy will only lead to problems and possibly to disruptions in collections management activities. Attacks on the policy, without practical suggestions, are counter productive. Staff must carefully examine the "canned" policy and test it against the reality with which they are familiar. This is particularly true for the registrar, who has a broader field of experience than most museum specialists and whose hallmark is the ability to solve complex problems.

The registrar brings day to day experience to the formulation of policy, holding up the lens of reality to abstract principles. How does the policy really affect the management of the collections? Does it carry out the purposes of the museum? Can the museum staff actually implement the policy directives?

If, for example, the policy requires fourteen file cards for each object in a collection of 25,000 (350,000 cards), the registrar can point out that this is clearly beyond staff capacity. This is a rational argument, something that the board will probably accept. If the registrar suggests how to handle the information requirements, all the better.

Despite lack of authority over the policy makers, the registrar can guide them by offering practical solutions to the problems. These solutions will probably be adopted. In this way, the registrar manages concepts, data, and the policy makers themselves. This skill will ultimately help the museum and the staff who work there.

Once the museum adopts a collections management policy,

the role of the registrar as its guardian grows more complex. The policy requires each staff member to act in a certain way. Making sure this occurs, and accounting for the tasks performed, are jobs that belong to the registrar. The role of the registrar changes from that of a scribe to a manager: the registrar becomes administrator for the collection, a responsibility based on the record keeping function and on expertise in the making of policy and procedures.

Procedures Manage Behavior

Museum staff have diverse interests and, in a large museum, work in different departments. Although registrars develop and manage the collections system, authority over personnel lies elsewhere. Yet the registrar must ensure that people—staff and others—carry out the collections management policy. For this to happen there must be procedures—step by step methods of carrying out the activities that policy prescribes.

Procedures are inextricably linked to policies. Procedures carry out policies; they imply and implement action. Policy makers often conceive of policy as providing guidelines and direction but neglect the practical matter of creating a system that ensures adherence to the directives. It is the procedural system that tests the validity and value of the policies.

Every policy, new or long established, has its strengths and weaknesses. If a new policy is ineffective, it will probably come into conflict with existing procedures or it will prove difficult to translate into new procedures: it will be an obvious irritant. If an existing policy is ineffective, staff will routinely ignore it. If a policy hampers normal activity, if it encourages errors in judgment, if it is too broad or too narrow, the registrar must diplomatically build a strong case with colleagues for its examination and revision.

Policy review refocuses staff attention on the museum's mission and nurtures a shared vision. The review will uncover policy directives that staff habitually thwart, and reveal unnecessary practices that have become part of procedural activity.

Even if not included in the original policy-making process, registrars invariably participate in the development of the procedures that concern collections. This gives the registrar a chance to use the human resources of the museum to develop an efficient collections management system. If policies govern behavior by telling staff *what* to do, procedures govern behavior by telling staff *how* to carry out policy directives.

Typically a procedure can be reduced to a set of steps. These should appear in a policy and procedures manual that anyone can consult. A procedure is often accompanied by a form that staff complete in order to initiate, record, or account for the steps or stages of the procedure. Simplicity is here a virtue— the fewer the actions and the shorter the form, the greater the likelihood that staff will follow the procedure.

To gain the cooperation of the museum staff the procedure must clearly be in the interest of the whole museum. This is achieved by identifying departmental requirements and by consulting with staff when developing or revising procedures. Cooperation is more likely if the number of procedures and forms is kept to a minimum and response time for action is short.

It is valuable to hold periodic reviews of procedures. This helps correct inefficiencies that have crept into the system. For example, an *ad hoc* solution to an old problem may have become an established practice even though it has outlived its usefulness. Reviews will keep the system lean and flexible: people will be more likely to use and endorse such a system.

Gaining support for the registration system is an important element in human resource management. User-friendliness is key: an intelligent lay person should be able to master the system. If the system is easy to learn, takes no great understanding to use, and allows secure, orderly access to the data and to the physical collection, it is effective.

People create the system, people use it. Long explanations of how the system works are useless; it should be self-evident. Inherent logic and simplicity characterize a congenial system that meets museum needs. The procedures, in this case, become self-enforcing and the registrar's skill apparent.

By understanding the purpose of a collections management policy and by carefully creating enabling procedures registrars enlist the museum staff to make the system work. The willing and active cooperation of colleagues is the ultimate measure of success in human resources management.

Communication

Museums preserve not only objects or specimens—the physical collection—but an intellectual collection. The significance of the physical collection is tied to an array of data. These may include cultural or historic or scientific context; provenance or origin; technique of manufacture, methods of use, classification, and interpretation. A record keeping system permits the development, maintenance, preservation, and dissemination of the intellectual collection. An object reveals certain attributes; the records do the rest.

The museum is an institution, expected to outlast any person. Since the museum survives the memory of the longest term employee, institutional memory resides in the records. When we examine an object record today, we in effect listen to the person who made that record. When we create a record today, we address generations of scholars and museum visitors to come.

Anyone who works with museum records learns about the people who created them, their little quirks, strengths, and weaknesses. Recorders become friends or enemies. This ability to communicate with our predecessors and with future colleagues is a fascinating aspect of the registrar's job. Just as curators create a collection that will remain long after they are gone, registrars create the records that will preserve the collection's history and intellectual richness. The registrar learns to understand past recorders, to communicate effectively with contemporaries, and to prepare records for future, sometimes even unknown, needs. In effect, registrars translate past policies and procedures for the benefit of colleagues today and tomorrow.

41

The registrar also communicates with the general public. This branch of the museum family often asks sophisticated questions. Queries about donations, identifications, and ancestors are typical. The registrar withholds judgment about the merit of the questions and responds quickly and accurately. Each answer can amplify the public support that is the life breath of the museum's existence.

Almost every question the public asks about the collection involves the registrar. The documentation that leads to the right object or the right answer is in the registrar's purview. Complete, accurate, and retrievable documentation reflects well on the system and the museum.

Trustees are part of the public too. Though they may be somewhat removed from the crowd, they represent the public in the museum's management structure. As a rule, trustees have a high opinion of the professional staff. Their trust is validated when staff can easily answer collections-related questions. Board members typically need statistical data (how many objects did we lend last year and at what insured value?) but they may also ask questions that require analytical judgment (how does the Pennsylvania Dutch dower chest under purchase consideration compare to others in the collection?). Registrars are habitually called upon to answer management's questions. They are required to answer promptly and their answers are expected to reflect the staff perspective.

The ability to communicate skillfully permits the registrar to act as an advocate for staff, indeed for the museum as a whole. Every time the registrar fulfills an information request from Jane Doe, from a prominent trustee, from a local third-grade class, or from a renowned scholar, the museum demonstrates that the staff controls the collection and the information about it.

The Registrar as Strategist

As evident by now, far from working solely with object lists and numbers, today's registrar is in constant contact with people. When communicating with the museum audience, the registrar fulfills a public relations function: sound information reflects positively on the museum. Internally, the registrar thinks creatively about the effect of the registration system on the daily activities of staff.

The registrar's influence goes beyond direct authority over assigned staff, budget, and facilities. The accomplished registrar knows that the policies that govern the registration system connect objects, information, and people. A truly useful registration system results in better collections care and in good relations among colleagues; it manages things, ideas, and behavior. In the modern museum the registration system is a multi-faceted strategy that answers the many needs of the museum staff and the public: the registrar is the architect of that strategy.

Note

[1]See, for example, G. Ellis Burcaw, in *Introduction to Museum Work* (Nashville: American Association for State and Local History, 1975), 40, who defines museum service personnel as "receptionists and clerks, handymen and guards, registrars."

Collections Management

Managing Collections Information

KAROL A. SCHMIEGEL

Registrars are in the information business. In the second half of the twentieth century—according to the trend analysts—that's *the* business to pursue.

Our society respects information and places a high value upon it. Universities teach information management, and information managers obtain increasingly influential positions. Information is the key to the modern economy. The craving for information, and the necessity to control it and make it work for us, have given birth to new technologies and disciplines. Consequently, our moment in time has been dubbed "the information age."

Information is unique in that it is both a resource and a product. Information is what we utilize to help us make sense of the world around us and the objects in it. Although the two aspects of information may overlap, the distinction is useful. In the museum setting, the differences between information as resource and product often stand out clearly.

Imagine, for example, that you have received a rather fanciful loan request. A historic house, only one hundred miles north of your museum, is planning a bicentennial celebration. Strapped for money, this small museum does not usually have all its rooms open, let alone adequately furnished. For this special exhibition, the director plans to borrow an elaborately carved 1742 Philadelphia card table. Information about the table is in your computerized database. It takes only a moment to call the information up on the screen and determine that the table needs treatment. In fact, the conservator has scheduled the table for the lab next month. This table is in no condition to endure even a short journey; and the thought of exposing the table to the possible jostling of a celebratory crowd would induce a coronary in the curator. The answer, then, is no. The information you sought, and received, has helped you make a decision. It has been a resource.

On the very same day, the curator of a small but highly respected midwestern museum calls you. A few years ago, this museum was the happy recipient of a choice private collection of early American furniture—with enough dollars attached to build a new wing. The curator is calling about object #1929.426.1—the same Philadelphia card table. She believes it may be one of a pair, and that her newly accessioned table is the mate. Her table was acquired from a Boston dealer in 1931. What information is available that will buttress (or undo) her hypothesis? A search for the provenance reveals that your museum's table came from the same eminent dealer, and was purchased one year earlier. Coincidence? Or was the original owner at first reluctant to part with both tables but ultimately persuaded to sell? (Alas, the original owner's name does not appear in the record.)

Your shred of information may be crucial to unraveling the history of the tables, particularly if the physical analysis of the objects reveals a kinship. At any rate, since your table is about to go into the lab, now is the time to put all the players in touch, so that they can share their findings. The information that you have just given the researcher is a product. It is something that somebody wants, something that (in theory, at least) could be bartered or sold. Your information and the researcher's hypothesis, brought together, may generate still new information, possibly of a very interesting kind. Perhaps even more will arise—not just about the genesis of the tables, but about how an eighteenth-century cabinetmaker went about his work.

This example gives some clues as to the nature of information. It shows how the nature of information changes according to how we use it. It also illustrates John Naisbett's contention that "unlike other forces in the universe, knowledge is not subject to the law of conservation: it can be created, it can be destroyed, and most importantly, it is synergetic—that is the whole is greater than its parts."[1]

Certainly the registrar's everyday experience confirms this view. What the registrar's experience also confirms—and what the tale of the Philadelphia table is also meant to reveal—is that second only to the objects themselves, a museum's greatest treasure is its data about the collections. Without this information, there would be no exhibitions, no catalogues, no tours, no programs, and no care of the collections. Without that resource and valuable product, the show would not go on.

A museum possesses and creates two major kinds of collections information. The first, *documentation* or *catalogue* information, consists of facts and opinions about the objects and specimens in the museum's collections. These are the data that interest the researchers: when was the object made; who made it; when, how, why, where it was collected; and who used it and how. The second kind is called *collections management* information. Management is the key term here. This information is what museum staff need to know before they actually do anything to the object; and it is what they record about the process. Moving an object from one gallery to another, lending it to another museum, photographing it, removing an unsightly varnish, are all activities that use and produce information. The two information functions sometimes overlap, and, in fact, the basic data that identify each unique object in the museum's custody are essential to both.

Museums do not all record data in the same way. But progress has been made towards standardization. In 1979, the Documentation Committee (CIDOC) of the International Council on Museums (ICOM) recommended that all museums record specific types of catalogue information. CIDOC proposed a standard to enable data exchange. The minimum is the name and address of the owner, the registration number, the object name or term, its category or classification, the mode and date of acquisition, the source and place of acquisition, and a description and history of the object. Although the categories are limited, they can be expanded to include others—the birth, death, and working dates of the artist; the names of former owners; and the credit line—information that traditionally appears in label text and exhibition catalogue entries.

Catalogue Information

Catalogue information is used in and generated by research and by examination of the object. Demographic data about the artist or maker, techniques of manufacture and decoration, the results of scientific analyses, traditions of ownership and use are all collections catalogue information, as are loan and publication histories, and opinions about authenticity and attribution. Subject matter and iconography, transcriptions and translations of text, also belong to the detailed body of collection catalogue information. Relationships to other objects, data about sites and recovery methods, correspondence with collectors, and researchers' notes become part of this documentation. Collection catalogue information, like other types of information, helps uncover more data, which is then interpreted and added to the growing body of information.

Museum documentation has its own peculiar demands. It is necessary, for example, to record some data as found (e.g., an inscription containing misspelled proper names) as well as recording data in ways that permit retrieval of the corrected version. Furthermore, because museums record not only the history of objects and specimens but the history of their documentation, it is necessary to add perpetually, rather than simply to replace old data with new. For example, in cleaning a painting attributed to Thomas Cole, the conservator discovers the signature of John Vanderlyn. The registrar corrects the records to indicate that John Vanderlyn is the artist but also retains the data relating to the former attribution. This is necessary for both scholarly and practical purposes. It will be many years before the corrected authorship becomes general knowledge, and people who request information from the museum about the painting will still refer to it as a Cole. Therefore, the museum cannot afford to "lose" the old attribution.

Collections Management Information

If you are planning to ship that Magritte back to Belgium, to exhibit those spectacular mollusks, or to scrub down that Rodin, don't—not until you get the right information!

The kind of data needed before undertaking any of these risky enterprises is collections management information. This information records any activity that affects an object, any transaction related to an object, and any movement of an object. Thus collections management information embraces a wide range of museum operations, including exhibition, accessioning, deaccessioning, conservation, loans, photography, and others. These activities both require and generate information. Various offices and departments within the museum contribute; all need the data to do their jobs.

Accessioning, for example, records the process by which an object becomes the museum's property: accessioning provides legal proof of ownership. The donor's name and address, date of the transaction, valuation or purchase price, and the source of funds are all part of the record, as are the appropriate credit line and any restrictions on the use of the object. Some of this information may find its way onto an accession list. In turn, the list may help the development office to identify potential supporters; it will also inform the accounting department of the value of gifts, and thus the amount of public support, information that an organization must have to retain its nonprofit status.

Deaccessioning is the process by which an object leaves a museum's collection. In the case of a sale, the records will account for the income received. Transfers to other public collections are recorded. Tracking changes in object locations, maintaining insurance records, scheduling conservation, photography, and exhibitions are all collections activities that require management. All generate and rely upon information associated with objects as they are used in museum programs.

Facts about crate size, dimensions of galleries and available storage rooms, the number of packers and preparators working on a given day, environmental requirements, and transportation schedules are facts required for smooth museum operations.

The management of this information parallels the management of key resources in the profit-making sector. The central management goal is an ambitious one: to acquire, maintain, and secure all the information that the museum staff needs to do its job, and to carry out the museum's programs. Authorized users need quick access to data, and the data must appear in a format appropriate to the task. Good data, well maintained, with easy and secure access—these are the elements that enable a museum to discharge its responsibilities to the collections in its custody and to its many audiences.

Planning an Information System

Randomly organized, haphazardly stored information, no matter how accurate, interesting, and pertinent, is useless. To be useful, information must be systematized; it must have a structure. Without a structure and system, there is no way to insure that all data are recorded or to know what is missing.

A system provides methods for storing information so that it can be easily retrieved. The system is the formal way of governing how the information is organized. It may be a special arrangement of material or a procedure. A system has scope, clearly defined boundaries, and organizational principles. A system is what makes a body of information into a functioning whole and gives it legitimacy.

Establishing a system for the immense variety of available collections information is a challenge. Catalogue information pertains to each object or specimen individually, but collections management information relates to the many operations and events that take place in a museum. The most familiar museum program, the exhibition, is a good example. An exhibition is a project: it has a beginning and an end. A record must be kept of the project, as well as of what happens to each object involved. The exhibition itself has a history, made up of all the activities that comprise the task. Everything must be tracked, recorded, and the results made accessible.

No two museums have identical information needs. Collections and activities differ just as the kinds and number of users do. Collections come in different types and sizes: a county museum that holds Civil War memorabilia will not process or systematize information in the same way as a large museum devoted to science and technology. The size of the staff, the ratio of staff to collections and programs, and the kind of training staff have received, are other determining factors in selecting or creating an information system that works.

Nevertheless, whatever the situation of a particular museum, or the idiosyncracies of its information needs, there are some basic guidelines an information manager should follow when creating or managing a system. Whether the system is manual or automated, the information manager (usually the registrar) will discover five major areas of responsibility: system documentation, user accessibility, data integrity, data retrieval, and data security.

An information system must itself be documented. A written description of the files and an explanation of how files are related are essential. Procedures for obtaining the information to create the files, and dictionaries of terms, abbreviations, and codes are important components. New employees and professional users require a complete set of instructions; the more casual visitors wishing to retrieve data need a simpler guide.

The information system also provides legal protection to the museum. Sanctioned policy is the bedrock upon which the information system is constructed. The policy describes the system's users: visitors or staff members, curators, exhibition planners, educators, development and public relations people. It outlines levels of restriction—who can see what information, who can change it. Depending upon the type of museum, the law may require public access to all information in a museum's records. However, the public usually receives information from printed materials, guides, or other media, and not directly from the museum's files. Scholars, students, and staff from other museums frequently request direct access to records.

Museum policy indicates who has what level of access to which files and when. Limited office staff and space typically mean that appointments are necessary for visitors to consult the files. Staff from some other offices may use some of the files after hours, and others may not. The museum may limit access to legal documents, such as deeds of gift. It may insist on the use of photocopies instead of originals for most kinds of study. Photocopying some types of records, such as invoices or artists' signatures, may be restricted or prohibited.

It is the information manager's job to insure the integrity of the data: the record aims to be accurate and current. The information manager ensures that every entry—initial and subsequent additions or emendations—bears the correct date. Changes to the information, especially valuations, locations, and custody require prompt notation. Information about additions to the collections should be available almost immediately.

To a great extent, the information manager is responsible for the accuracy of the data. Facts and opinions coexist peacefully when distinguishable. Furthermore, an information manager who has knowledge about the museum collection serves as a questioning reviewer. The registrar is not always expert in every area of the museum's holdings, but must recognize fundamental errors. If a 1735 engraving is catalogued under "wove paper," the registrar should note the inconsistency. If the inscription "kyrie eleison" is said to be in Latin, the information manager should recognize the language as Greek. In addition to correcting such inaccuracies, the information manager administers standards of format, of terminology, and of timeliness.

Information is meant to be useful, and to be useful it must be available. A well-structured system provides efficient retrieval of data and makes it available in the form desired by the user. The format may vary. Information can arrive orally, as in a reply to a telephone inquiry, or in writing, as in correspondence, lists, file cards, and publications. A photograph or slide, a microfiche, a computer printout all constitute forms of information and are accommodated into information systems.

Staff responsible for collections records must know the access policy to insure confidentially. They must also know how to care for the records to reduce the effects of wear and tear. Records must be safe from theft, fire, and other disasters. The museum should have off-site storage to house duplicate sets of records as well as a copy of the system documentation. An effective collections information system will protect sensitive and confidential data and will be physically secure.

To be effective a system does not have to be complex. The goal should be to make the system as simple as the complexity of the collection allows. Meeting the normal needs of the user is a good criterion for evaluation, but as users and needs change and expand, the information systems should be able to do so, too.

Why is all this activity necessary? Museum data are valuable intellectual property. Museum data support collections care and all other museum programs and functions. Increasingly sophisticated audiences approach museums with heightened expectations and knowledge. They expect a wealth of experience from "leisure" activity. Museums are accountable for the property they hold in public trust. Both audience expectations and administrative awareness of legal and ethical issues have increased the scope of data management responsibility.

For registrars, this change implies that their province is extending its boundaries. There is more to do and, with the advent of new technologies, more ways to do it. Whether managing information for a small historic house museum, for a zoo, or for one of a handful of mega-museums, registrars experience unprecedented demands on their time, on their expertise, and, most of all, their ingenuity. The information age is upon us, with all of its new blessings, tribulations, and rewards.

Note

[1]John Naisbett, *Megatrends* (New York: Warner Books, 1984).

The Registrar in the Cabinet of Curiosities

MARGARET SANTIAGO

A natural history museum is a world unlike any other. The direct descendant of the Renaissance "cabinet of curiosities," the natural history museum still astonishes the visitor with its unusual specimens and the variety of its collections. Plants, snakes, lizards, birds, animal bones and skins, shells, fishes, worms, shark teeth, fossils, gemstones, beetles, butterflies, and sometimes Indian arrows, potsherds, and mummies fill the display cases and line the walls. Even in a specialized natural history museum that devotes itself exclusively, say, to gems or butterflies, the visitor gets an impression of the vast profusion and mystery of the natural world.

Behind the scenes, a natural history museum continues to fascinate. The research library may contain eighteenth-century botanical texts just a shelf away from the latest journal articles. In the lab, a visitor might find an entomologist measuring the curious nests of African dirt termites, or a geologist peering at crystal formations through an electron scanning microscope. The storage areas contain countless drawers of animal bones collected in remote gulches of the American southwest; in the cabinets stand orderly columns of specimen jars holding dead-eyed fish. (The aromas of mothballs, alcohol, and formaldehyde attest to the fragility of some of the specimens, which must be carefully preserved.)

All of this is stimulating, and piques the imagination, but it may overwhelm even people who work their whole lives in such museums. Certainly the variety of specimens, and the sheer numbers of them, present challenges to the person entrusted with record keeping: the registrar.

Collections Management

Among museums, it is the natural history museum that boasts the largest number of collection specimens and artifacts. Whereas only the largest art museums hold more than a million objects, it is not uncommon for mid-size museums of natural history to hold several million. (The largest art museum in the United States, the Metropolitan Museum of Art, has an impressive three million; but its counterpart in the sciences, the National Museum of Natural History [NMNH], holds 118 million and a single department there may acquire over half-a-million specimens yearly.)

These enormous quantities of specimens arrive from all over the world. Some are gifts, others result from oceanic and field expeditions to foreign lands. There are archaeological digs and projects that the museum staff initiate, and collaborative ventures with other institutions at home and abroad. In all cases, laws govern the collecting, importing, and exporting of specimens. Furthermore, expeditions and scientific inquiry result in requests for identification and the analysis of materials—yet another area of responsibility for a natural history museum.

Collections typically reflect the varied disciplines of science that trace the heritage of mankind, biology, and natural resources. It is usual for collections to be dispersed among several scientific departments. (At the NMNH these departments are anthropology, botany, entomology, mineral sciences, paleobiology, vertebrate zoology, and invertebrate zoology.) Scientific departments traditionally collect, document, study, preserve, and exhibit specimens, and also collaborate with the registrar who tracks, monitors, and records what happens to the specimens as they move within or out of the museum.

Even museums that devote themselves to one scientific discipline, or even a subset, face immense tasks. Collecting, describing, studying, and cataloguing North American beetles, for example, is no small endeavor. In museums with complex collections the work is multiplied. Individual departments interact and exchange information, and also function as mini-museums and research centers. Administrative procedures and record keeping must facilitate access, not hinder it, and must reflect the needs of curators, technicians, researchers, and the public.

A registrar in a natural history museum, especially a large museum with many collections, is often frustrated. The inclination of any registrar is to categorize, to enumerate, to clarify. In a natural history museum, some collections, by their very nature, defy the registrar's *raison d'être*. Try counting a sediment sample! Or pot shards! (At least distinct entities, these can present an insurmountable barrier to enumeration: does fragment number A18739 belong to pot 2022 or pot 2026, both being painstakingly reassembled, or to neither?) For such collections, the registrar records batches or lots that fit the requirements of the registration system and that facilitate scientific inquiry.

There are additional classification hurdles of overlapping categories. When a specimen or object turns out to have significance for more than one scientific discipline, the registrar may have thorny problems to resolve.

Natural history museums share characteristics with other museums. They hold specimens and artifacts that are of interest principally to researchers while other artifacts have tremendous public appeal. Some artifacts are extremely portable and have high monetary value (a celebrated diamond, for example) and require impregnable security. Certain specimens and objects call for meticulous handling, carefully controlled temperature and lighting conditions, and specialized preservation treatments.

All these factors help shape the registration policies and procedures that staff must follow. Sometimes policies and procedures are seen as onerous; at other times, staff regard them as the means to bring order to ever-impending chaos. For if there is a general characteristic that typifies natural history museum collections it is one shared with other museums: very little ever leaves the collection. "No growth" is unthinkable, particularly to the scientific disciplines that thrive on discovery and build on previous knowledge. Inquiry demands growth, constant exploration.

What is it like to work in such an environment? What does the registrar do when faced with a constantly expanding universe, difficult to comprehend, impossible to master completely? What demands are there on the registrar's skills? The job requires an overall knowledge of how the museum operates, the ability to resolve conflicts, and a flair for investigative research, for tracking a wayward specimen or an elusive fact. An instinct for potential disasters, administrative and legal, is also helpful, as is a cool head. Most of all, a registrar in a natural science museum must have an understanding of what will best serve the interests of the museum—both the "inner museum" of scientific research and the "outer museum" of public programs.[1]

Some real-life examples serve to illustrate the complexity and excitement of the registrar's job. What are some of the situations and people the registrar encounters? And how does the registrar cope?

A Day in the Life of . . .

One sunny morning, the registrar arrives at work to find a parcel post delivery on her desk; the box originated in Montana. The neatly typed label addressed to the museum indicates no curator, no department. This is an unsolicited donation, of which there are countless examples every year.

Inside the box the registrar finds feathers—and a note from someone who collects Indian curios, who wishes to donate these to the museum. Nothing about the origin of the feathers, or how they were collected. No value indicated. Nevertheless, these feathers cannot remain on the registrar's desk. After a few judicious phone calls, the feathers—some loose, others still attached to shreds of leather, possibly a headband—still do not have a home. Instead a full-scale imbroglio unfolds.

Not surprisingly, the feathers are intriguing to the ornithologist. Some specimens suggest that a raptor, not known to have ever ranged so far west, may well have been common there 150 years ago. No one had ever considered the possibility:

maybe this is the start of a new investigation. "The feathers were probably acquired by trade," snaps the anthropologist, who has been studying Indian trade routes across the American continent. "Besides, I'd like them for my department because I suspect these feathers were used in a religious ceremony." This is not merely interdepartmental rivalry: there are good reasons to assign these feathers to both departments for study, and in fact, both departments will examine and describe the specimens, and arrive at separate, possibly related, conclusions. Nevertheless, the feathers must somehow enter the museum records, and the records should include the salient facts about the feathers. But what are the salient facts? And how are the feathers to be categorized?

Another complication arises. The ornithologist discovers the feathers of two different raptors among the specimens. He insists that several of the feathers are new: "Why, these could have been collected *yesterday*." An ardent protectionist, he's fuming: "What about the Migratory Bird Act?" He's right. Someone is going to have to look into how the bird feathers were collected. It's illegal for a private party to possess even one feather of a protected bird, and the museum has to report possible felonies. The curator and the registrar will confer on this, and one of them will call the U. S. Department of the Interior's Fish and Wildlife Service.

The story of the unsolicited donation could be spun out further, but surely the point is clear. One donation alone can bring the registrar a multiplicity of dilemmas. In this fictionalized example, the registrar has had to deal with specimens that may have been acquired illegally, not to mention the problems of ownership that will undoubtedly surface. The system that the registrar maintains must be rigorous and flexible enough to reflect and accommodate all these variables. It must balance viewpoints—scientific and administrative—and require resolution of conflicting concerns. It must record the process as well as the solution; this is especially important when legal matters arise as the museum may be required to demonstrate that it works in accord with the laws that regulate collecting.

The last point is worth underscoring. Though only specialists master the intricacies of the laws, curators and registrars must keep an eye out for violations. In the example of the illegally acquired feathers, it was the Migratory Bird Act that provoked action on the part of the registrar. The Endangered Species Act and the Marine Mammal Act are two more laws familiar to the vertebrate zoologists. When it comes to other disciplines, say paleobiology, a whole new set of regulations apply. Fossil collectors, particularly those not associated with institutions, are not always careful about claims of ownership after digging. A generous gift from a collector, or even a find made by the museum staff, can involve the museum in a costly, time-consuming legal tangle. It can even turn into an international incident. Here is another example to illustrate that point:

The young botanist has had an exhilarating morning. He has just gotten off the phone with a curator in Mauritius, and it looks as if his trip to this remote island in the Indian Ocean is going to happen. What luck to have struck up a conversation with this enterprising colleague at the international conference on the Index Seminarium! The botanist and an American team will get a chance to explore the unique insular environment of Mauritius, and the university museum researchers there will get the opportunity to examine the American museum's specimens. The Mauritians are eager for this loan—rare specimens of their own native flora, collected years ago by American field botanists, specimens stored for several decades.

Impetuously, the botanist rushes in to see his department head. He tells her the good news: the university museum in Mauritius is ready, willing, and able; it's all lined up; they're even interested in doing a special exhibition; he will submit a travel request shortly. "Why that's wonderful," says the department head, adding, "Don't forget to clear the loan procedure with the registrar."

The registrar! In the excitement, he had let this slip by. He knew he had to notify the registrar that this collection was slated for loan. It shouldn't take long; he decided to run down to the registrar's office before going to lunch.

The registrar's office is filled with file cabinets. A couple of computers blink away. A secretary sits at the front desk. He asks the secretary for "one of those forms . . . I'm arranging a loan." "I think you will have to see Miss Smith," says the secretary, "she will want to ask you some questions."

What did the registrar ask the botanist? There are policies and procedures that govern what the poor botanist, feeling quite besieged, had to answer.

The first thing the registrar wanted to know was the accession number of the collection. The botanists didn't have one. He explained that he had looked through the departmental files looking for "purely scientific information." "You didn't happen to see a reference to an accession memorandum in the files?" the registrar asked again. No, he hadn't. "So you don't know if these specimens were ever accessioned?" asked the registrar. "I assume they were," said the botanist, "They were just sitting there in storage." The registrar made a mental note and went on with her querying. "Where were the specimens collected?" "In Mauritius, obviously," answered the botanist, trying not to sound peevish. "Have the Mauritians sent you a letter requesting the loan?" Actually, no. He had done all the negotiating over the phone. He was going to need a letter of intent from the institution in Mauritius. Were the facilities there equipped to safely house the specimens? He assumed they were—he would have to find out. The registrar would provide a facilities report form to help the botanist ask the right questions of the borrowing institution—questions about safety, security, handling and exhibition procedures. Were the specimens fragile enough to require a courier? Yes, and he intended to do it. Had he already pulled the collection? Yes. Where were the plant specimens? In his office in their boxes. Was that a secure area? (The botanist was beginning to feel uncomfortable.) Did the plant specimens require any special preparation before they go out on loan? Did he, for example, have any special packing or handling requirements? "And are you familiar with the laws governing such loans?" added the registrar.

The registrar and the botanist established a cooperative relationship and began detective work. After searching both the registrarial and the curatorial files, they ultimately pieced together the history of the collection. Some of the Mauritius specimens had been collected in the 1930s by a botanist from the U.S. Department of Agriculture; the wild grains had been transferred to the museum's collection just before World War II: they had been duly accessioned. The rest of the specimens had been taken out of Mauritius by a team headed by a researcher from the American museum in 1973. The researcher, who left the museum shortly thereafter, deposited the specimens in storage, with the earlier specimens. He left a rudimentary paper trail in the curatorial files. This second group of specimens were never accessioned, never officially entered the museum's holdings, and for good reason. Some of the specimens were covered by legal stipulations that required return to the government of Mauritius. Ownership resided with the people of Mauritius, represented there by a government agency. Apparently the curator of botany at the university in Mauritius, who hadn't known of the 1973 expedition, had gone along with the botanist's assumption that the American museum owned the plants.

Now it became the joint responsibility of the registrar and the department of botany to see that proper action occurred and proper documentation followed. Ultimately, some material entered the collection of the American museum, and some returned to Mauritius. The Mauritians and the Americans arrived at a joint agreement as to the disposition of the collections and subsequent research access. The small exhibition of rare flora took place at the university in Mauritius and a team of American botanists explored the island and collected more specimens. No international incident, no law suits, no bad press, no embarrassed museum directors.

Though museum staff may sometimes feel that they are enduring the third degree, it is the responsibility of the registrar to ask the questions—some obvious, some not so obvious. The registrar is charged to protect the museum, and to pay close attention not only to the in-house procedures but to the implications of any activity that involves moving an object or a whole collection. Legal matters loom large, especially if they involve international transfers or loans. There is a lot of room for misunderstanding when dealing with another culture or another country's regulations. Furthermore, a loan always entails the cooperation of many different people; the registrar strives to anticipate the concerns of scientists and packers, scholars and customs agents, foreign governments and the museum's own general counsel. Moreover, many public inquiries funnel through the registrar's office.

"I'm looking for a dinosaur," says the voice over the phone. Alas, the owner of the voice doesn't know what kind of dinosaur. He just knows it's a *whole* dinosaur and he traveled all the way from Richmond to see it. That was five years ago. He wants to bring the grandchildren to see the dinosaur; where can he find it?

The museum displays eighteen dinosaur skeletons and several models. The registrar writes a letter to Mr. Jones in Richmond and obligingly includes postcards of the dinosaur models. This is beyond the call of duty, but it should make Mr. Jones happy. (The museum is partially funded by Mr. Jones' tax dollars and he deserves individual attention.) Unfortunately, this does not satisfy Mr. Jones. He calls again: the postcards were useful, he says, because now at least he knows what he's *not* looking for. The photos have helped him remember more: the dinosaur he wants is lower to the ground, and has "things" sticking out of its back.

The registrar is stumped. There is no such animal in the museum. Leaving the building later that day, she becomes aware of a horde of school children swarming over the dinosaur model on the lawn. It's a large lumpy dinosaur, low to the ground with peculiar ridges down its spine. Previously part of the landscape, she wonders now, could this be it? If so, why isn't the dinosaur model in the accession files? It is a lawn ornament of dubious scientific value, but it is a model, probably ordered and paid for by the museum, and it does—doesn't it?—belong to the museum.

She calls Mr. Jones. "Why, of course," he says, "it was out-of-doors!" How could he have forgotten? "How could others have forgotten?" mutters the registrar. She calls buildings and grounds and she calls the department head in vertebrate zoology; she calls education and public programs. Somehow, some-where, someone either ordered this dinosaur or accepted a do-nation, and had it plunked down on the lawn. And where are the records?

The records, intact, with an attached (but never filed) acces-sion memorandum, were found on a shelf four years later. The prime mover in the dinosaur project had left the museum years ago. It took numerous calls and a lot of investigation to figure out which departments had been involved. Actually, the records were in fine shape; it was simply that no one had ever taken the final step of carrying the file over to the registrar's office.

What does this example illustrate? It shows how, with the best will in the world, some things fall through the cracks. This is not an admission that most museums would care to make, but it is nevertheless true. In this case, the absence of records on the lawn dinosaur was a startling omission: the model was very popular with the public—it symbolized the museum. Be-cause it was not strictly scientific, no one bothered to finish the project after the project manager left. After all, public programs generally do not generate collection items. They can, however, bring the scientific message to the visitor. Everything belongs, and everything must be accounted for.

How One Museum Does It

The National Museum of Natural History (NMNH) in Wash-ington, D.C., is one of the treasures of the Smithsonian Insti-tution. With its millions of specimens it offers unparalleled research opportunities.

Most people assume that this collection is completely computerized. Not so. In fact, the size and scope of the collection, combined with a growth rate of nearly a million specimens a year, defy current technology.

Meanwhile, the manual registration system continues to handle the movement of a staggering number of specimens, artifacts, and documents. In 1986, for example, new specimens entailed 1,542 accession transactions. Mollusks, fishes, birds, gems and minerals, worms, crustaceans and amphibians, reptiles and mammals, ethnological and archaeological specimens all found their way into the museum collections.

In addition to what comes in, the system handles what goes out. There are transfers and loans to U.S. government agencies, particularly to the Interior, Agriculture, and Commerce departments. These agencies have their own research efforts and laboratories, and engage in cooperative work with the museum. There are exchanges with other institutions—universities, for example—and scientists. There are loans, for research and exhibition, to other museums, and even to foreign governments. Close to 183,000 specimens left the museum as loans in 1986, accounted for in 1,857 transactions by the registrar.

Of course, those simple categories—things that come in and things that go out—are deceptive. Some specimens and artifacts are outright donations or bequests. Others are loans, for research and exhibition. Some are there "on approval"—specimens that the museum is considering for purchase or exchange. Others are the result of field trips or expeditions. Yet others are sent by other institutions or private individuals for help in identification or analysis. Furthermore, items that leave the museum also go out for complex purposes, and under different kinds of agreements. All this needs to be accurately recorded. Returned loans, unsolicited donations, and specimens and artifacts sent for identification, are likely to arrive directly at the registrar's office. Due to the heavy volume of incoming specimens, the complexity and special handling requirements, most collections go directly to the curatorial unit of a specific department. It becomes that unit's responsibility to inform the registrar of arrivals and dispositions.

The policies and procedures of each department have much in common, but they differ according to the specific requirements of the collection. In each unit, curators, technicians, and specialists share collections management responsibilities; ease of handling and safety of the specimens are paramount. Specimens are packed, stored, and preserved with varying techniques. Some specimens are preserved in dry boxes, others in liquid solutions, still others in special chambers. Staff must know how to handle chemicals and plastics, how to make casts, or how to retrieve a collection of vole carcasses from Siberia.

Recently arrived collections undergo examination and collectibles are separated from noncollectibles. The noncollectible material may be debris from a dig or dive, duplicates, type specimens that must be returned per loan agreement, or material of inferior quality. Noncollectible material might be used for teaching purposes. Some materials, such as human remains, may be returned.

If a bird or mammal skeleton is wanted for the collection, the specimen undergoes skinning, followed by cleaning in a bug chamber. Specialists examine the skeleton for acquisition following the cleaning process. Therefore, agreements cannot be finalized until the process is complete.

Donations of meteorites from recent falls require immediate attention. It is important that scientists take measurements as promptly as possible and that they analyze the meteorites prior to contamination by the earth's atmosphere. Rapid storage in nitrogen gas prevents deterioration from exposure to oxygen and water.

Fossils—that range from protists (one-celled animals that can not be seen with the naked eye) to dinosaurs—are typically imbedded in rock or sediments. Just getting at the specimens is a tough job. Fossils may receive an acid bath to eat away the matrix and prevent the growth of gypsum.

Collections management in any single department is equivalent to collections activities in a small science museum. The chair of each scientific department serves as the administrator and manages collection activities. Each curator is an authority for a particular collection. Specialists, technicians, and aides support the scientific staff and assist with collection handling and documentation. Other staff, such as clerk-typists, secretaries, and fund managers who handle accounting and procurement, are also assigned to departments. In some departments there are divisions. For example, the department of invertebrate zoology includes the divisions of crustacea, worms, echinoderms, and mollusks.

A manual registration system is the nucleus of heavy collection activity. The movement of collections in and out of the department requires a documented system of policies and procedures that relate to registrarial methods, to oversight and control, and to the museum's overall purpose.

Each day the registrar receives requests for registration numbers from the divisions. In the case of incoming collections, the departments forward the original documents to the registrar, who assigns and stamps the registration number on the documents and all supporting papers. The registrar then begins an information log, containing the name and address of the sender, the date of the original forwarding document, the type of transaction, the kind of specimen or artifact, and the title of the responsible in-house unit. The registrar prepares an index from the information log.

During the registration process, the registrar prepares a receipt for the staff members to sign upon release of the documents. Thus the unit retains all the original, now registered, documentation. The registrar maintains the log sheet, the index, and the receipt until the specimen disposition is completed by the department. When the curator decides the disposition, he or she then prepares an accession memorandum (if the specimen is to enter the museum's collections) or a shipping invoice (if the specimen is being returned or transferred elsewhere). In either case, the documents go to the registrar.

The registrar also assigns numbers to outgoing shipping transactions. Specimens or artifacts leave the museum as loans, as exchanges, or as transfers. Collecting and scientific equipment may also leave the museum, sometimes as loans to other institutions or perhaps for repair. The mechanics of the registration process are important. Like information belongs together, and the flow of information must be smooth and logical. Staff must adhere religiously to the procedures; otherwise retrieving the information becomes haphazard, and the integrity of the system is destroyed. As with automated systems, staff use key words and phrases—receipt, registration number, category, kind of specimen, date of transaction, catalogue number, incoming, outgoing, and disposition—as stepping stones for orderly search.

In a manual system, it is essential for the registrar to have an alphabetical file of index cards for outstanding transactions in the departments. The index cards, filed under the sender's last name, include the date of correspondence, kind of specimen, type of transaction, and the responsible unit of curation. Once the registrar pinpoints such information in the register, the curator or specialists should be able to ascertain the location and status of any collection within reasonable time.

As in museums of other types, large natural history museums often support two levels of record keeping, registrarial and curatorial. The registrar controls information about incoming collections and captures key information about accessioned material. Registrarial action begins upon notification that a collection is to arrive in the museum. All documents are reviewed for accuracy prior to entry into the museum's record.

The curator, on the other hand, records and documents each specimen or artifact. This involves cataloguing and recording descriptive data about the specimen's race, age, genus, and family, as well as where it was collected. The curator records information on identification, condition, conservation, and storage location and compiles documents relating to loans for study, exhibition, specimen distribution, and accessioning; and the curator also credits donors and lenders.

The size and complexity of the collection will dictate the number of persons responsible for registration activities, and the degree of system centralization. Heavy collection activity generates thousands of documents. Updating existing accessions, loans, and shipping files, is a never-ending process.

Files may be centralized in a registrar's office or decentralized to the curatorial level. In either case, documentation requires close scrutiny. Procedures and safeguards must be in place to maintain high standards for documenting information and to protect the system.

Coordinated shipping, receiving, and registration of collections generally creates a greater capacity to oversee movement, to monitor adherence to museum policies, and to capture data. Furthermore, centralized collections information systems aid research and promote sound management. Auditing departmental documents and procedures helps maintain uniform, consistent methods of documentation. Audits help assure adherence to museum policy and orderly procedures; this is basic to maintaining the museum's legal status as a public trust.

Much of what a registrar does is aimed at safeguarding the museum. The endless battle over the facts that appear in the record represents the creative, dynamic tension between a scientific community that is forever exploring and redefining boundaries, and the administrative community (here represented by the registrar) that needs tangible, retrievable information in order to serve the public and to fulfill legal obligations.

Accountability is a top priority in the registration system. Documentation must be both flexible and rigorous—often opposing goals. A system can insure accountability only if people use and understand it. Training, of both registration staff and staff of departmental units, must take place regularly. It is the registrar's responsibility to see that this is done, and that all who come into contact with the system understand its importance, its governing policies, and its quirks.

Staff must feel comfortable with complex procedures, a high volume of shipments, loans, accessions, and complicated insurance policies. Training sessions permit the registrar to educate new staff members, remind existing staff of how the system works, and attempt to eliminate confusion by interpreting and clarifying policies and procedures. The training session also becomes a forum for discussing the system's short-comings, and for suggesting improvements. Proper guidance for collections management personnel is a must for maintaining order in a diversified institution.

The registration staff receives training of a technical, detailed nature. They must also learn "people skills," for much of their work entails face to face or phone contact with many different clients. They must know, for example, how to handle walk-in visitors. Being helpful and courteous while simultaneously securing museum records requires tact, sound judgment, and a knowledge of the policies and procedures that govern the use of permanent files.

The staff of the registrar's office must be adept at fulfilling research requests. In the registrar's office at NMNH, it is not unusual to receive upward of one hundred such requests every week. Scientists, writers, reporters, and relatives of donors are among those who visit or call on the registration staff for information. The registration staff also handles calls from the public about collection policies that govern donations and loans, and about the location of specific types of collections.

The registrar's office also answers questions from the museum staff. Generally, staff wish to know how to carry out various shipping, accessioning, or deaccessioning activities. They also often need information or statistics related to the distribution of specimens or to other matters under the office's jurisdiction.

The registrar of a natural history museum must juggle responsibilities creatively and manage a system that inspires confidence in its users. The registrar must understand system definition and be thoroughly at home with the museum's collection management policies and procedures. The registrar should be able to review documentation and spot potentially trouble-some ethical or legal issues. Expertise in financial management, records management, and administration is indispensable. Finally, the successful registrar is someone who is adaptable and open-minded, and has a good grasp of the nuances of human behavior. The bottom line for survival while managing a large natural history museum system is to be knowledgeable, congenial, and flexible.

Note

[1]Philip Humphrey, Letter to the Editor, *Museum News* 65, no. 1 (October/November 1986): 5–10.

How the West Was Hung: A Corporate Collection Tour

ELIZABETH CUNNINGHAM

*M*asterpieces *of the American West* is an exhibition that began a six-year tour of the United States in 1983, traveling to more than twenty venues. A selection of paintings from the Anschutz Collection (collected by Philip Anschutz and owned by the Anschutz Corporation), the exhibition traces 150 years of American history and culture. It reflects the lively appeal of the West to the artists who visited or made their homes there and provides insights into this country's westward expansion.

As the corporate curator of the Anschutz Collection I was responsible for organizing the show. This meant that I assumed the mantle of project manager and began carrying out duties usually assigned not only to curators but to registrars, educators, administrators, and public relations specialists. In all of this I had the help and guidance of the collector. Nevertheless, all aspects of the exhibition—from initial concept to the safe return of the works—were my responsibility. While to the museum visitor, *Masterpieces of the American West* offered the delight of discovery, to me the exhibition was a lesson in management.

The Tasks

Organizing an exhibition for travel in the United States is a complex undertaking. All the classic aspects of project management come into play. But what do planning, budgeting, and implementation mean when applied to a traveling exhibition?

When I translated these terms into specific tasks, the result was daunting. The list of things to do included:
- defining the content of the exhibition
- establishing a budget
- selecting exhibition sites
- negotiating contracts
- developing promotional and educational materials
- public relations
- fund raising
- collaborating with exhibition site staff
- packing and transportation
- risk control and insurance purchase
- inventory and condition review

I was to discover that these activities do not necessarily occur in chronological order. Some tasks, like public relations, have to be done during the whole life of the exhibition, and may even continue till well after the exhibition's close. Other tasks, like collaborating with exhibition site staff, have to be done repeatedly. Many things that appear settled are not. Budgets, for example, are subject to revision. And unexpected occurrences can bring the manager back to the first step of what was a supposedly final game plan. For example, if a museum pulls out of an exhibition schedule at the last minute, the project manager must alter not just the schedule, but the budget, the travel arrangements, promotional materials, and more.

Nevertheless, *Masterpieces of the American West* did develop in an orderly way, and followed a more or less prescribed blueprint. Let's examine this development step by step.

Exhibition Concept

The first step for me was to try to look at our collection with fresh eyes. What were its salient features? Its strengths? What would draw the public? What would pique the imagination? If

I were new to western art, what would I want to see? What would strike me as unusual, interesting, unpredictable?

When I sought to answer these questions, the features of the Anschutz Collection that most struck me were its richness and variety. The collection boasts over seven hundred pieces, predominantly paintings. The paintings range from Albert Bierstadt's *Rocky Mountain Waterfall* to George Inness' *Afterglow on the Prairie* to Helen Frankenthaler's *Phoenix, 1976* and Chuck Forsman's *Dirt Rider*. The collection eloquently expresses a regional experience and a significant American aesthetic.

The scope of the collection suggested the exhibition concept: to convey the unfolding and development of the American West as interpreted and depicted by successive generations of artists. Such an exhibition would also reveal much about the history of American painting and manifest the collector's vision.

To embody the exhibition concept we sought an image that would convey both the harsh realities and the mystical qualities of the American frontier. A careful review of the collection turned up *Pueblo of Taos* by Victor Higgins. The artist's rendering of traditionally garbed Pueblo Indians drenched in the bright, white light of New Mexico gave life to the exhibition concept.

Pueblo of Taos became the foundation upon which the exhibition concept rested. The image appeared on all graphic promotional materials—brochure, press kit, poster—as well as on the exhibition catalogue. Not only did the image express something fundamental about the American West, but the quality of the painting became a standard for the selection of the other works of art.

Choosing the Works of Art

The collector and I chose the works of art painstakingly. In our review of the paintings, we asked the following questions:

- What is the quality of this work? Is it one of the artist's masterworks?

- What will the viewer know after looking at this work?
- Does the painting convey a sentiment or a feeling of time and place?
- How does the painting reflect the environs of the West in which the painter was working?

What we were seeking were paintings that expressed the era in which they were created, paintings that conveyed a vivid sense of western life and that also made a strong artistic statement. Our questions helped narrow the field.

The next step was to create a representative balance. Pictures were deleted because one genre was over represented, or because too much attention was paid to a particular artist, school of painting, theme, or technique. The remaining paintings were considered and reconsidered, always in the light of the exhibition concept: Did the artistic vision tell the viewer something about the development of the West?

Ultimately, the collector and I selected eighty paintings to tell our story. The selection was broad ranging and of high quality; it could satisfy the most stringent curatorial standards.

Interpretation

Each of the works chosen for exhibition had artistic merit and could stand on its own. Nevertheless, the subject of the paintings communicated the phases of westward expansion, and seemed to call for contextual material. Such material would assist museum staff and enrich the visitor's understanding of the art and history of the American West.

Exhibition labels gave the artist's name and dates, the title and date of the painting, its medium and dimension. In addition, labels provided a brief biography of the artist, a description of the painting's subject, and comments on the place of this painting in the artist's *oeuvre* as well as its relevance to life in the West.

A catalogue presented a more complete picture of the works in the exhibition. The catalogue included color plates of significant works and introductory essays written by me and by a scholar of the American West. A map and a historic time line allowed the reader further entry into the period.

Aspects of the West alluded to but not discussed in the catalogue were treated in supplementary educational materials. The materials supplied information on such diverse subjects as artists' colonies and Indian rituals; also included were bibliographies of films, literature, and photography. Intended for museum staff, the materials were useful in docent training, school programs, and curatorial research.

Audio-visual presentations were another way to add meaning to the museum visit. We developed a slide show depicting the people, places, and events of westward expansion. Slides of the paintings in the exhibition were complemented by pictures taken by local photographers, and images from collection and photo archives. In addition, a twelve-minute video was produced for gallery use.

Promotional Materials

Finding exhibition sites around the country was a high priority; but we could not market the exhibition to museums without first developing promotional materials. These materials—a brochure, a poster, and a press kit—accompanied the proposals made to museums during site selection. The press kit included the exhibition schedule, a painting checklist, a list of available photographs, an exhibition abstract, and several reviews of an earlier show.

Planning

It took two years to plan the exhibition. Much of this time was spent in site selection, which entailed consultations with museum directors, curators, registrars, and public affairs personnel. The preparation of interpretative and promotional materials was also time-consuming. Among the specialists consulted were scholars, photographers, printers, publishers, designers, and producers of audio-visual materials.

An important part of planning is to re-evaluate ideas. For

instance, we decided to dispense with wall text panels and maps—
initially considered basic to interpretation—because exhibition
spaces were so dissimilar. (This also gave museums greater
freedom in designing their exhibitions.) Even the content of the
show underwent refinement: we removed some paintings because they proved too fragile to withstand travel; we added
some new acquisitions.

Planning, it must be remembered, is useful insofar as it
orders the known universe. If properly conceptualized, a plan
will accommodate the unpredictable opportunity—such as the
purchase of a new painting or an unexpected donation of funds.
A plan also minimizes crisis management situations that can be
disastrous to irreplaceable works of art and can strain even the
most cordial working relationships.

Budget

Money. How much? From where? When will it be available?
These questions underlie any exhibition. Quite early in the planning process, we discovered that in order to formulate a realistic
budget we had to establish financial policies.

Our policies clarified our budget picture. We decided to
charge no rental fee, thereby placing the exhibition more easily
within the financial reach of each museum. In addition, the
Anschutz Corporation advanced funds for catalogue production;
the catalogue was sold to museums at cost for resale to the
public. The corporation funded production of the brochures,
posters, postcards, and press kit covers, and recovered the cost
from museums on a per piece basis. The corporation paid outright for audio-visual production, conservation, framing, crating, labels, and inventory and storage of the catalogue and graphic
materials. Museums paid pro-rated shipping costs, insurance,
in-house overhead, and, if they chose to hold an opening reception, its costs.

Accurate budget estimates are essential if the exhibition is
to go forward smoothly. An unexpected cost overrun is the last
thing a project manager needs. Key budget items include trans-

portation, insurance, and production costs for promotional and educational materials.

In order to estimate the budget for graphics, I canvassed various museums to gauge average use or sales of the catalogue, postcards, posters, press kits, and brochures. I multiplied these averages by the projected number of exhibitions over a two-year period. The anticipated quantities were increased to accommodate additions to the exhibition schedule. This method took advantage of economies of scale, kept costs to the museums reasonable, and consequently lowered the price to the public.

Transportation is a major expense in any traveling exhibition's budget. It is important to examine the collection's transportation requirements in some detail. *Masterpieces of the American West* traveled by road—a method often safer and easier to control than shipping by air. Bids were solicited from trucking firms with established experience in the transportation of fine art. The bids required exclusive use, air ride trucks with environmental controls, and two drivers. Even though exhibition contracts had not yet been signed, city time tables permitted the project manager to estimate the costs accurately.

A budget item with important ramifications is insurance. Since loss and damage to collections is most likely to occur in transit, insurance must be adequate to the risk. This is no time to cut corners. The total value of the traveling exhibition, derived from current appraised values, was submitted to the collector's fine arts insurance carrier. Insurance premiums were established on a wall-to-wall basis for a two-year period. Each museum paid insurance costs from the time the exhibition arrived until safe delivery at the next venue. The Anschutz Corporation advanced the costs and billed the museums on a per diem basis.

Site Selection

Once the exhibition content was decided, and the groundwork laid for the budget, it was time to market the show.

We began by identifying major urban museums with diverse

83

audiences as exhibition sites. We placed phone calls to the directors of the proposed museums, and followed up by sending them notices of the availability of the show, as well as the budget, graphic material, catalogue, and press kit.

Some museums responded enthusiastically; others rejected the show. Time and space limitations were factors; in some cases, the collecting and exhibition mandates of the museum excluded the subject; some museums did not exhibit private collections. But positive responses were plentiful, and the exhibition opened at the Portland Art Museum in September 1983.

Sponsorship

Once the initial two-year tour had been booked, we attempted to find a sponsor for the entire exhibition tour.

Two corporations—Mobil Oil and United Technologies— seemed likely prospects. (They had previously sponsored a European tour of works from the Anschutz Collection.) United Technologies declined because it had already designated funds for an exhibition of similar subject matter—*The American Cowboy*. Mobil Oil, however, agreed to partial sponsorship and decided to fund exhibitions in four cities where Mobil had corporate offices. Mobil underwrote the exhibitions at the New Orleans Museum of Art, the American Museum of Natural History in New York, the Museum of Fine Arts in Houston, and the Oklahoma Art Center in Oklahoma City.

We assisted the other sites in their search for funding. Each museum eventually found sponsors, due to the quality, popularity, and broad appeal of the exhibition.

Communicating with the Host Museum

The project manager of a traveling exhibition works with the departments at the host institution. Curators and registrars, public relations staff and educators, all take part in making the exhibition a success. All departments play vital and separate, though frequently overlapping, roles in the exhibition process.

In my experience, establishing communication with the individual departments within a museum was a difficult challenge. The immediacy of the exhibition process, combined with the heavy workloads endemic to museums, tended to overload the lines of communication.

By trial and error I discovered that the best way to communicate was through written correspondence that was then copied and distributed to the departments. Verbal communications were frequently documented and distributed in this manner. All communications emphasized what the museum could expect of me (and the corporation I represented) and what we required of the museum staff. Eventually, form letters were developed that further improved liaison.

Communication has to work well because so many things have to be done, and done quickly, to make an exhibition, any exhibition, a success. From the time a museum commits itself to an exhibition, to the time the objects leave the premises, both the project manager and the museum staff have their hands full. I have found it useful to codify the procedures for dealing with the host institution. As the procedures gradually become second nature, there are more opportunities to think about the exhibition's creative aspects and to share ideas with colleagues. Here are the procedures for *Masterpieces of the American West*:

How It's Done

Soon after a museum commits itself to the exhibition, I contact the curatorial department and forward the catalogue and press kit. I also send a questionnaire that asks for a description of the museum's general operating procedures, as well as the names, titles, and phone numbers of all the staff with whom I'll eventually work.

Three to six months before opening, I send the curator the exhibition checklist, with frame dimensions. Supporting materials on historical and art historical subjects accompany the checklist. (This information is critical to those designing the

85

exhibition.) I contact the public affairs staff and send them a press kit, and a list of color transparencies and black and white photographs available for media reproduction. Once a time table is set, the public affairs office receives all the press kits, posters, catalogues, and brochures it needs to promote the exhibition.

As the date of the opening draws nearer, I have more and more contact with the public affairs staff. As the press becomes increasingly interested in the exhibition, I find myself fulfilling interview requests and forwarding additional documentation.

The public affairs staff and I decide what image to use on the invitation to the opening, but my involvement stops there. The department manages the opening; staff draw up the guest list and determine protocol.

Two months before the opening I contact the education department. I forward materials that will assist the educators in creating programs for both children and adults. The subjects range from Indian customs to photographers in the West. I also send a list of relevant books, films, and seminars. The slide show and video tape are made available.

Two months before opening, I send the registrar the exhibition checklist, the crate list, and the details of shipping arrangements. The registrar needs to know where the shipment originates, the name of the shipping agent, the name of the registrar at the preceding site, how the crates were packed, how much storage space the crates require, and whether any additional material accompanies the works of art. Once the collection arrives at the host museum, the registrar is its custodian. The registrar provides logistical support and is responsible for noting any changes in the condition of the objects.

Closer to arrival, I inform the registrar of any additions to or deletions from the exhibition. These may occur because of damage to a work of art, cyclical conservation routines, a superseding loan commitment, or the acquisition of a work that ought to be exhibited.

A week to ten days before opening, the paintings arrive. The registrar reviews their condition and notes any changes in the condition report book that accompanies the objects. If any painting has sustained damage in transit, or if any deterioration is apparent, the registrar notifies me. I am the only person who can authorize conservation or replacement.

The next step is installation. With the arrival of the exhibition begins an intense cooperative effort: the curator, the registrar, the exhibit designers, and the preparators go to work.

Unless the host museum asks me to design and install the exhibition, these responsibilities belong to the staff: they are familiar with the exhibition space and audience, and can thus do the best job. (If requested, I advise on design and installation.) As is customary, I reserve the right to make changes to the installation. Usually, changes are not required; but if they are, such changes are negotiated with the installation staff until consensus is reached.

Shortly before the opening, I arrive at the museum and meet the personnel who so far have been only telephone acquaintances. My role in the opening varies; it may include docent training, media interviews, and gallery lectures.

At the opening reception, I meet the membership and answer questions about the works of art. As the representative of the Anschutz Corporation, I greet the sponsor. Frequently, a private celebration follows the reception, allowing me to cement relationships with the sponsor and the museum staff.

Masterpieces of the American West spends one to three months at each venue. During that time, the museum becomes the exhibition's guardian; standards of care and security are expected to match those that the museum accords its own collections.

Toward the end of the exhibition tenure, I contact the registrar to arrange shipping to the next destination. I tell the registrar of any deletions and give separate transport instructions for works pulled from the show.

When the paintings are taken down from the walls, the registrar examines them and records changes in the condition report. The next step is to re-crate the works of art and supervise the loading of the crates into the transport vehicles. The exhibition then leaves the host institution to travel on to the next site. The project manager and the registrars of both the old and new venues verify the safe arrival of the exhibition. And the process begins again.

Corporations and the Arts

The success of *Masterpieces of the American West* illustrates a synergistic exchange between the business and museum worlds. Increasingly, the vitality of museum exhibitions in the United States has become dependent on business corporations. The private sector is a major collector—with collections available as loans—as well as a major sponsor of exhibitions. Corporate management realizes that sponsoring exhibitions helps project a quality image. Enlightened corporate leaders recognize the parallels between the creativity of the arts and sciences and the creativity demanded by the challenges of business excellence.

Many corporations take quite seriously the ideal of being or becoming responsible corporate citizens. Today's employees are interested in quality of life issues, and want to know that the company for which they work is contributing to their community. Pride in the work place contributes to productivity. Support of museums is one way to instill that pride and to guarantee positive community involvement. These are the ideals behind *Masterpieces of the American West*.

Moving Imagery: Collections Management During a Museum Move

GINGER HENRY GEYER

The director is on cloud nine. Two weeks ago he announced to his staff the successful conclusion to negotiations that had been dragging on for over a year. Yes, the museum is finally moving! Its new home will be the former Masonic Temple just off Main Street, and one of the best architectural firms in town (conveniently headed by a trustee) is about to begin the renovation. The present museum building, with its dimly lit galleries, its over-flowing specimen cabinets, its cramped little lab, its makeshift photography studio, and its inadequate security, will soon (well, relatively soon) be a distant memory. The director has quit breaking pencils . . . but why then has the curator suddenly taken to viciously biting his nails during meetings? Why has the registrar preserved a funereal silence since the announcement? As for the conservator! She has been yelling nonstop at the bewildered intern for the better part of the week. The move is good news? Isn't it?

America's museums are growing. Not only are new museums springing up, but established museums are renovating galleries, building additional wings, or moving into totally new facilities. Behind this activity lie shifts in population, redistribution of wealth, and new forces in collecting. As museums change to fit the needs of the public, and to care for their collections, one phenomenon occurs over and over again—the relocation of museum collections.

A relocation is a challenge for any organization, but the special needs of museum collections make a museum's relocation particularly difficult. A museum move involves many phases:

planning, preventive maintenance, shuffling collections, packing, transportation, unpacking, installation, and adjustment. Each of these phases presents unique problems and opportunities. For museum staff, a move can feel like an uprooting—something violent and unpleasant. But a properly managed move, with full staff participation, is a revitalizing experience.

Organizational Growth

A major move—one that involves a total relocation or substantial expansion—will transform the internal character and public perception of the museum. Though a museum is much more than bricks and mortar, the activity generated by the new space will force the institution to grow. Such quantum leaps are rarely made without numerous adjustments; and the more compressed the expansion period, the harder it will be to manage the consequences.

Students of change, such as Theodore Caplow, have documented the symptoms of discontinuity during growth: the breakdown of organizational norms, internal theft, obsolescence of some long-time staff positions, increasing dependence on outsiders, and the realization that familiar procedures no longer work.[1] A museum may experience some or all of these during a move.

Staff attitudes are bound to be vividly expressed during such a time. After staff learn that the comfortable and familiar patterns are going to change *no matter what*, some predictable responses will follow. There will be the inevitable period of disbelief and procrastination, then the realization that "Yes, we are moving." A conscientious, fastidious professional staff will have real and imagined fears with which to deal. For those in collections management, there will be the fear of public scandal (reporters exposing the dark, dank storeroom and unfinished inventory records), the fear of personal liability (dropping a box of Oriental porcelains), the fear of errors in judgment (miscalculating the time required to move, or causing cost overruns) and the unspoken fear of not being needed in the new setting. Imaginary chaos may reign, with such phantom headlines as "Sculpture Rapes Painting in Museum Freight Elevator." And curators concerned about too much publicity are only half-joking when they suggest that all crosstown moving be done at dawn in plain white vans labeled "Zippy's Fried Pies."

As staff scrutinize the long-overcrowded and somewhat disorganized storerooms (the result of years of more pressing priorities), real fears begin to surface. Someone will now have to deal with that smelly trunk full of artifacts that have never been accessioned or individually registered. Then there's that numbering discrepancy embedded in the 1940s sequence—what will that do to record keeping during the move? Does anyone recall the one specimen missing from a group of ten? And how will movers safely extract that huge old painting, the one that's partly hidden behind the storage bins that were built during the growth emergency of 1963?

It is understandable that moving a collection may arouse only limp enthusiasm, the eagerness usually reserved for cleaning out the junk accumulated under the bed. Some resistance is a normal response. But when too many major surprises are suddenly introduced in a dictatorial manner, resistance to change can manifest itself in more harmful ways—sabotage, rumors, power struggles, withdrawal, and hostility.[2] On the other hand, optimists will emerge and begin to spread the word that moving can be beneficial; they may even suggest that it will improve matters. Though a positive attitude is certainly helpful, fantasizing will lead to later disappointment.

It is critical that supervisors deal with the psychological impact upon the staff throughout all stages of the transition. After all, the safety of the collection is directly affected by the behavior of the people who handle it. Management must let staff know that a major relocation is a large-scale project, bringing both transitory and permanent change. Everyone must understand that the project does not end on the day the collection arrives at the new site, or on opening day of the fancy new wing or the splendidly appointed new building. The move is a long transition period that begins with an initial planning phase and continues through an evaluation period some months after the opening of the new facility.

An early evaluation of the museum's readiness for change will pay dividends. It will allow the future scenario to develop in a structured way, with input from all staff levels. Planning the expansion is a job for everyone, and staff should help develop, or at least give their opinions about, space allocation, adjacency diagrams, and blueprints. When they turn from this task to the actual move itself, staff will need a reserve of energy to draw upon; they will need inspiration.

There exist standard management formulas for dealing with rapid organizational growth. One that might serve a museum in the planning stage of a move includes:

- team management
- decentralization of operating responsibilities
- standardization of procedures
- centralization of financial control
- expansion of communication facilities[3]

This method of managing a move is not as bookish as it appears. Team management permits the museum to maintain existing operations while supervising the expansion. There will probably be a period during which the old museum has to keep up a good front and function as usual, while behind closed doors the disruptions of the move are taking place. A move team or task force needs to control both settings.

A team of senior staff members with administrative responsibilities should include at least one person with responsibility for the collection, someone who can serve as coordinator of the collection move. This project manager should not have to carry on the continuing activities of loans, exhibitions, and processing new acquisitions. A major relocation project deserves its own management. Decentralization simply means delegating tasks. It requires a clear chain of command, since a management

94

team without sufficient authority will only confuse subordinates, especially in times of rapid growth. The move manager must attempt to standardize procedures and establish priorities.

During a move, staff and administrators are running what amounts to two organizations, the old museum and the new museum. This can have a disastrous effect on the budget, especially if there is a construction cost overrun. Tight, centralized financial controls will help avoid this pitfall. Finally, adequate communication is critical when staff is decentralized and two buildings are in use at the same time. This may be the time to expand communications networks. After the move, informal patterns of communication will require some time to rebuild, so it helps to establish formal communication methods well ahead of time.

Planning

Planning the collection move requires considerable "give and take" among staff. It is helpful first to outline realistic goals and to back them up with objectives. One goal, for instance, might be "to move every collection object without damage or loss." If this goal is truly realistic, the objectives that follow should specify object-handling procedures and foolproof record keeping methods.

Every move has its milestones—the construction deadline, the opening date—and elements that remain more or less constant, such as the budget, staff time, available space, and the number of collection objects. Although nailing these down in advance helps to set goals and objectives, remember that everything is subject to change. It is important for staff and administrators to recognize the need for flexibility and to agree on how much flexibility is appropriate for any given target.

Next, it is very helpful to devise a project flow and time table. The project flow is a detailed list of steps leading towards the goals. This document serves both as a checklist and a means of gauging progress. It helps keep the project moving along in the right direction at an acceptable pace.[4] The project flow might outline 30 or more steps in the record keeping process, perhaps organized in phases—"pre-move," "during the move," and "after the move." For each step in an activity, personnel must be assigned and chronological bench marks anticipated.

The point of the project flow is to predict complications and to work through them. But, however careful the planning, there will always be unexpected snags: that's why flexibility is fundamental to museum renovation projects, or to moves tied to the completion of a construction. Rigid adherence to the plan may sometimes be counterproductive. For example, don't insist upon first moving and unpacking all display objects (the plan recognizes the time crunch of the installation staff) when construction delays have made those galleries inhospitable to objects. Such inflexibility could lead to damaged objects. In addition, logjams can result from such unquestioning adherence to established procedures. The move team must recognize when these procedures don't work, and tailor its approach to the realities of the situation.

Inevitably, there will be times when staff will have to lower their professional standards; they may find this hard to accept. For instance, staff may have to pack some objects early and hold them aside to save space and time. Budgetary constraints may dictate the use of less expensive, nonarchival packing materials. Perhaps a compromise is possible—by selecting less valuable objects, by revising the budget line item for supplies, or by reworking spatial uses and schedules.

There may also be a tendency to over-plan the move, hoping that this will prevent problems. The amount of minutiae to cover is overwhelming; and anxiety may exaggerate the importance of anticipating *everything*. No one can predict precisely what will happen during the transition, and no one can control external circumstances. The project plan, therefore, is a realistic but imperfect tool and those who follow it must recognize its limitations.

Carefully planned and controlled change in one area of the

museum can cause unexpected pressure in other areas. For instance, though the collection move itself may be meticulously worked out, planners may have overlooked the moving of unassociated furniture, fixtures, and equipment; and problems suddenly spring up in the assemblage of museum library shelving or in the storage of membership brochures. These hitches are every bit as distressing to those departments as the collection move problems are to registrars.

The accumulation of various problems creates widespread stress and can result in interdepartmental competition. One way to lessen competition is to encourage regular and unambiguous communication between museum departments, in the form of both meetings and memorandums. This is critical if the move involves the sequential closing of galleries and public areas, since this will affect the work of all other departments—education, public relations, membership, and development as well as the museum shop, restaurant, and building maintenance and security. It is unfair to the docent program and to the public at large to say that "the museum's American galleries will close whenever we need to pack the objects in there." For the education department to demand that those galleries remain open beyond a reasonable date is equally unfair. One way of minimizing staff stress is to provide "creature comforts" during the move period—a makeshift break room, an occasional meeting held in a park, a catered box lunch in the construction zone.

Scheduling

During a move, scheduling becomes a fluid activity. If a museum chooses to use a large planning chart it should be easy to alter. (Wall calendars with erasable surfaces or magnetic strips for long and short-term tasks are helpful.) Use a sliding calendar system in which definite bench marks act as controls and weave more flexible activities in and around these bench marks. Bench marks such as "early opening for education wing, November 11–18," or "conservation consultant in town for examination of textiles, late November," or "garden party for twenty-five hundred capital donors, December 7" are all valid deadlines to use in the schedule.

There are many ways to schedule packing, moving, and unpacking. One approach, which helps to predict exactly when work will occur, and divides this work into manageable segments, is to pack, move, and unpack one group of objects at a time. For instance, pack, move, and unpack all ceramics, or all tools in storeroom number six, or all objects scheduled for the opening exhibition on nineteenth-century American technology. Another way to handle this is to decide on separate schedules for each of these three activities. The condition of the new structure will help determine the approach.

The most frustrating roadblock will be construction delays; and sudden announcements of delays by people other than those working on the collection move is another irritant. It is important for the move coordinator to be well informed about the construction progress: the completion of plumbing, air conditioning, heating, and humidity controls will influence the decision to move the collection in or not. These construction milestones, and the completion of security and fire systems, painting, and flooring should be part of the collection move schedule from the very beginning. As completion dates change, moving activities will also change. A conservator familiar with environmental and construction hazards should evaluate building readiness. It is a fortunate museum that does not have to sacrifice conservation standards in order to open on time.

Workspace

Juggling the use of existing space in the old facility is another challenge, especially in a crowded museum undergoing renovation. It may take some creative thinking to set up a temporary packing area, holding area, or photo studio. Sequential gallery closings may be useful, as galleries often provide the only available work or storage areas. The built-in casework in the African section, now vacated, may make very handy shelves for neighboring objects awaiting packing. The large contemporary art gallery may do quite nicely for re-rolling tapestries. Turning galleries into temporary working quarters requires logistical skill; pieces once displayed have to be stored or packed in advance and location changes recorded.

An alternative is to rent warehouse space. This avoids the hazards of construction dust and workers, but its drawbacks include excessive moving, more expense, and risks with security, inventory control, and environment. Moving collections back and forth from off-site holding areas can be as perilous and unpredictable as shuffling the objects around the in-house construction hazards.

Budget

Developing a budget is a major step in planning any special project. This process occurs during the planning phase. The nagging uncertainties of the move may make budgeting difficult, so a generous contingency line item is critical. Primary expenses may include:

- outside labor (mover, packer, conservator, photographer)
- temporary staff positions (preparator, inventory help, data entry clerks)
- supplies, equipment, vehicle purchase and rental
- computer time or software development
- insurance
- rental of storage or workspace

If the move coordinator is held accountable for expenditures, he or she must also have the authority to monitor and revise the move budget. A special project budget is a notorious hiding place for expenses vaguely related to the project. Redirecting staff time away from usual activities may save some labor costs but will necessitate programmatic changes and will add to backlogs. Supplementing staff with volunteers is a good option if volunteers are dependable, well trained, closely supervised, and assigned to routine tasks. Another way to save dollars is to buy packing supplies in bulk and to solicit donations of acceptable materials and equipment. (Some of these can be recycled or used in the new facility.) The museum's fund-raising or development officer may be able to obtain donated moving services—useful only if the services are precisely what the museum wants.

Publicity, Security, and Insurance

Publicity, security, and insurance coverage all affect collections handling. Most museum moves have public appeal: what local newspaper can resist shots of loading a truck with raging mastodon models or Van Goghs? It is wise for the move team and public relations staff to prepare early. Draw up a "publicity wish list" of objects accessible to the media, and begin negotiations.

It is unwise to move delicate pieces, or those that have previously caused anxiety (for example, a recently broken sculpture) under any but controlled circumstances, with no observers to ask questions, get in the way, or otherwise interfere with concentration. Yet media coverage of routine packing and moving can rouse the interest of the community, and can be beneficial to the museum during the semi-closed phase. Report news of the move *after* the move itself has taken place. (It will jeopardize security to announce in advance precisely when the museum plans to move the jewelry collection.) The moving vans should not be conspicuously marked; neither the vans nor the museum's loading dock should appear in the press or on television in recognizable form. No one should disclose the value or insurance premiums of objects, specific moving dates, or details about the security systems. The media are under no obligation to edit. Letting them know in advance what they can expect will help to sustain their interest, and they will probably appreciate a prepared statement from the public relations department.

Others curious to see what a museum looks like behind the scenes during a move will include well-meaning trustees, staff, volunteers, and donors. Letting these people in on the move may be important to the museum's livelihood (to a trustee, the visit may be a legal obligation), so it is best to set aside times for visitation—times when objects are not "touchable" and when anxiety is not high. The move coordinator should advise the director on appropriate times for visitation, and the director in turn should exercise control over trustee inspection during sensitive procedures. The move coordinator must instruct persons entering off-limit areas about the rules. It is probably wise to restrict photography and to prohibit talking to staff members at work. It is essential to restrict the touching of objects or equipment. Visitors should also wear identification badges and understand that contracted workers may not know who they are or why they are VIP's. If the museum does not have a badge system, there is no better time to start than before a move.

The chief of security must participate in planning all aspects of the move, for this will be a time of vulnerability, with many opportunities for theft. Old and new facilities for storage and transportation may all require more guards and more electronic surveillance. There should be controls in effect on freight elevators, docks, storerooms, and galleries. For crosstown transportation of high-value items a follow car with radio communication may be necessary. Some shipments may require police support. Careful thought should be given to fire prevention in packing areas; a ton of tissue paper and ten foot stacks of cardboard boxes are very real hazards.

The museum should contact its insurance agent early to discuss coverage during the move. Some companies restrict the monetary value of each truck load; others, informed in advance, waive such restrictions. Even with such a waiver, it is wise to avoid concentrations of value or like objects per load. (Here again, computer-sorted lists can assist in planning.) Insurance for the new facility should include collection coverage effective as soon as objects enter that space. This may mean paying an extra premium if the museum is occupying both buildings at the same time. An early estimate may convince move planners to reduce this interim period or to increase security, or both. The decisions of the insurance company can thus have an effect on scheduling as well as budgeting.

Movers

The choice of labor for packing, moving, unpacking, and installing objects will make the biggest impact on the budget. Securing the best help possible—from existing staff, temporary hires or professional movers—is worth the effort of redirecting funds or raising money. Of all budgetary items, labor is not the one where scrimping saves. Some museums, however, have completed well-executed moves with volunteers or unpaid workers.[5] To be successful, amateur labor must be closely supervised and well trained by museum professionals who have hiring and firing authority.

If the museum is able to hire extra hands for packing or moving the collection, it is important that the choice be formally conducted. The museum should solicit bids from moving companies that it has used before or that come highly recommended. Don't just consider local companies; out of state movers do not always have prohibitive prices. Opening up the bidding process, however, is a waste of time, as it attracts companies ill-suited to a job that requires special expertise. Exercise caution when dealing with overconfident household movers; they may try to convince you that they can handle a museum move because they "are used to moving valuable antiques and sensitive electronic equipment."

A detailed request for proposal (RFP) is a good vehicle for obtaining responsible bids. The museum staff should carefully prepare this document and send it out to those companies on the bidders list. Components of the RFP should include:

General Conditions of the Job
- the scope of the work
- the categories of property to be moved
- the necessity for a site visit

- the museum's move team
- the mover's role in planning
- what the mover should furnish
- protection of property and structures
- coordination with construction crews
- timing
- security and the method of moving
- insurance payments
- payments to mover
- liquidated damage

General Qualifications of Bidders
- proven experience in packing and moving comparable objects
- experienced personnel
- use of subcontractors

Inventories
- collection objects by type
- noncollection objects

A good RFP is also useful for donated services, or even if the museum plans to use its own staff, because it serves to document expectations. Presenting the details in advance will save time by discouraging unqualified movers from bidding. It is important to eliminate all unqualified candidates early in the process. Some government-supported museums may have no choice but to award the contract to the lowest bidder; therefore, only the top contenders should make the final round.

The museum should require all qualified bidders to visit the site before submitting bids. This inspection should take one or more days and include tours of both new and old facilities, storage, galleries, and dock areas. Members of the move team, curators, and conservators should "quiz the bidders" to judge their expertise. Always check references! The selection process may take several weeks—give bidders ample time to line up subcontractors and to prepare written bids. The bidding price should not be the deciding factor; expertise and confirmed references count for more. Inexperienced companies may grossly inflate their bids to cover a large margin of error, or they may miscalculate the scope of the project and underprice their services. If the best movers for the job submit a high bid, negotiate before eliminating them for cost-cutting reasons.[6]

Once the museum selects the mover, the contract is negotiated and reviewed by the museum's legal authorities. The contract incorporates the scope and details of the work as outlined in the request for proposal and any other terms agreed upon with the movers. A procedure manual and a training session by museum staff will be valuable for both professionals and inexperienced helpers. The movers should agree to participate in this and to abide by the museum's rules.

Inventory

Moving a large collection is an easy way to lose inventory control, not to mention individual objects. After the move, the only assurance that all objects were successfully relocated is by crosschecking the premove inventory. A museum can move its collections without a prior inventory, or it can conduct inventory simultaneously with the move—the state of the museum's inventory records will dictate the better way. If possible, it is advantageous to conduct the inventory in advance and with the move in mind, as this will accomplish much more than the standard verification of locations and accession numbers. Collecting such information as condition, size, handling restrictions, preparation needs, materials of composition, and generic object type reveals much about the collection. Tabulations of this data simplify estimates of truck loads, supplies, labor, and time. Use of inventory data can save thousands of dollars as it allows the professional movers to submit a bid very close to the actual cost of the move.[7]

It would be impractical to tabulate inventory data manually, even for as few as one thousand objects. A well-designed computer system is an invaluable tool for any such project, and for a collection move a computer can combine inventory results more effectively than twenty registrars armed with an infinite supply of index cards. A computer can generate such useful lists as: "objects in storage lacking identification arranged by location"; "top conservation needs according to curatorial area"; "small ceramics requiring mounts for new installation"; "oversized objects requiring large van"; "decorative arts sorted by area, object type, and size for cabinet storage"; "fragile objects to be moved only by conservators." Inventory will also ferret out overdue loans and abandoned property in storage. The museum should come up with a strategy for dealing with such objects before the move. Inventory information can also assist with logistics and help identify projects to be done in advance. It will also bring to light major needs to be scheduled after the move, such as a comprehensive conservation treatment plan based on generalized condition information collected during inventory.

Record Keeping

The methods for keeping track of the collection during the packing, transportation, and unpacking phases will vary from one institution to another. Nevertheless, any record keeping system should include: timing, labor, number and types of objects, objects that can be grouped for moving, objects needed by staff and scholars during the move period, readiness of the new facility, and types of final reports required. Time-savers that can improve record keeping include a designated location for each object and well-marked, well-prepared storerooms and galleries at the receiving end with storage units and display cases ready for use. It would be ludicrous and irresponsible to move the collection without determining general installation and storage sites beforehand. Staff will need space and time to regroup objects prior to packing, in order to lessen handling at the other end where facilities may be less familiar and temporarily more crowded. Generate new facility location lists by entering individual projected locations into the computer; lists can be used to verify arrival. Or, similar objects can be loaded, transferred, and put away in a shelf-to-shelf correlation—much like the move of a library, with varying degrees of reorganization. It saves time and space to customize moving vans and carts for carrying several similar objects at a time. Delivering grouped items to the same new area can also speed record keeping.

During the period of the move there may be the need for access to objects for research or installation planning. The record keeping system should be able to accommodate this, but such requests should be made in advance to prevent excessive object handling. It is difficult to predict where bottlenecks in the record keeping will occur, so a test run is a good idea. Computers can produce stick-on labels, cards, check-off lists and formal shipping documents to cut down on paper pushing, inaccuracies, and duplication of effort. The computer can also expedite proofing of new gallery labels by manipulating collection data for those labels and producing a backup copy for direct typesetting. Finally, the computer's ability to compare the pre- and post-move inventory is a huge time-saver.

The use of computers for record keeping and project tracking is the single most profound change recently introduced in museum moves. A large project like moving a museum collection can justify obtaining a computer system, especially since the system will be useful later. Planning for a move must begin well in advance and so must the planning of software needs. Coordination of the two projects will result in more cohesive record keeping and better use of the computer. It is essential that the computer system provide rapid data entry and updates, and be capable of broad retrieval. Once software is in place, a test-run of the record keeping procedures is advisable. This will help solve problems in both manual and automated systems. Once moving begins, telecommunications or mobile terminals can save time, especially if collections occupy two or more sites simultaneously. It is important, however, that the move of the computer itself not disrupt the flow of record keeping on objects in transit.

Other Opportunities

Perhaps the biggest benefits of a collections move are the improvements to location control and care of the objects. A move can give rise to other projects as well. It provides a rare opportunity to clean house and get rid of unnecessary objects. A household move may result in an estate sale; a museum move may spark major deaccessioning. The controversial nature of deaccessioning decreases when disposal of objects occurs in conjunction with a move: deaccessioning become a prudent and necessary housekeeping action. It is an unusual collection that does not contain abandoned property and undesirable acquisitions. Such objects require as much attention and space as the rest of the collection, and this costs the museum money.

An estimate of the cost of maintaining objects will help justify deaccessioning unwanted items. To determine cost allocation, first identify the givens—such as the wages of collections management personnel. Consider the wages of other personnel, such as guards, maintenance staff, and administrators who all devote time to collections management. Include direct costs, one-time costs, and fixed costs—supplies, moving equipment, collections insurance. Determine percentages of costs for space use—utilities based on cubic feet, building insurance, repairs—and itemize them. Different methods of allocation yield different calculations, but an overhead rate can be convincing. It is a good exercise, too, as it puts a price tag on behind-the-scenes efforts.

Moving also gives the museum a chance to improve its manual and visual documentation. Few museum collections are fortunate enough to have total photographic records, but the risks of a move are an incentive to document the entire collection. Basic documentation photographs or videotapes may be enough for insurance purposes, but it is better if the photographs have usefulness that goes beyond the move. Cataloguing, too, may improve as curators write gallery labels for previously unexhibited pieces and find long-forgotten objects in storage.

Conservation will be the area hardest hit. Despite the best of efforts, handling always endangers objects. There are opportunities, however, to improve the conservation program. More objects will receive condition reviews and some never scheduled for treatment will receive it in order to withstand the move and the reinstallation. The need for preventive maintenance will surface vividly as years of neglect become apparent: paintings vibrating in loose, ill-fitted frames; works on paper suffering mat burn; creases in improperly stored costumes. The first close inspection of that smelly old trunk may result in a fumigation effort or conservators may decide to fumigate whole truckloads at a time. (Remember that contingency line in the budget?) Finally, the move may also bring about a greater awareness of object-handling techniques if staff members interact with professional movers. The contracts with riggers, crane operators, and other sub-contractors may likewise prove beneficial in the future.

After the Move

A museum should welcome a move because it provides opportunities for needed change. After the move, the museum should plan to take these improvements out of the project stage and integrate them into the mainstream of the museum's life. Good collections management must become routine. One path to this goal is to obtain priority status for collections management in the museum's long range plan. If such a plan already exists, staff should reevaluate it with current collections needs in mind. Projected growth in collections, exhibitions, scholarship, publications, and education influences the use of collections and hence their care.

If the museum has not done so, now is the time to draw up a collections management policy, followed by a procedures manual. The new museum will suffer growing pains, and these documents can help the staff to adjust. The new setting will require changes in procedure and the temptation may be to bureaucratize before these changes have time to surface. Working through the adjustments can be annoying, but it is a real part of this final phase.

Because staff behavior affects collections management, guidance of staff through the aftermath is an imperative. If staff have depleted their energy by moving and installing the collection they should not have to face a new exhibition program the very next week. Nostalgia for the old place may develop as unrealistic expectation dwindle. Now is the time to encourage postponed vacations and to minimize new activities; otherwise, staff burnout will occur.

A museum move may at times look like a symphony playing without a conductor, but the opportunities it affords can override the problems it causes. A move is a major step in the life of a museum and should receive all the care and attention that corporations give to changes in primary assets. Moving a museum collection demands advance planning, careful monitoring, expedient problem-solving, creative policy-making, and thoughtful risk-taking. It can move the collections management process to maturity.

Notes

[1]Theodore Caplow, "Change," in *Psychological Foundations for Organizational Behavior*, ed. Barry M. Staw (Berkeley: University of California, 1983), 407.

[2]This point is emphasized by William Maynard, "Skills Managers Need to Survive," *Administrative Management*, December 1982, 70.

[3]Caplow, "Change," 408.

[4]Lenore Sarasan and A. M. Neuner, *Museum Collections and Computers* (Lawrence, Kansas: Association of Systematic Collections, 1983), 66.

[5]Shelly N. Reisman, "Moving Policies: Conflict or Resolution," Paper presented at the annual meeting of the American Association of Museums, San Diego, California, June 10–14, 1984. The Tennessee State Museum used volunteer packers and a group of prisoners to move the boxes.

[6]Larry Francell and Ginger Geyer, "Specification for the Move of the

Dallas Museum of Art," November 9, 1982, 1–7. Government or corporate procurement regulations may preclude negotiating with a vendor after an RFP has been let without giving all the other bidders the same opportunity. One purpose of an RFP is to allow vendors equal opportunity.

[7]Prior to moving the new Museum Support Center, Smithsonian Institution, collections were inventoried and data used to help determine the number and kind of storage hardware units required. A premove inventory at the Dallas Museum of Art provided collection statistics so close to the actual job that the move project was completed on time and well within the budget.

Thinking Simply

CAROL O'BISO

In 1982, as chief registrar of the American Federation of Arts (AFA), I went to New Zealand to begin logistical research on an exhibition of Maori art. I was accompanied by a conservator, and it was our goal to lay the groundwork for *Te Maori: Maori Art from New Zealand Collections*, an exhibition scheduled for a 1984–85 tour of the United States.[1] My responsibility was the care and handling of the works of art—in this case, in New Zealand and at each of the four venues to which the exhibition eventually traveled in America. It was my job to address and resolve all the issues pertaining to packing, transportation, insurance, climate control, conservation, and fumigation as well as to establish the standards of care for the handling of the objects throughout the tour.

Te Maori proved to be a very special exercise. This was the first international exhibition devoted exclusively to Maori material and all 174 objects came from the country of origin. Only a handful had ever left New Zealand; most had never left the wall or storage chambers of their museums. Only one person from the American side, the guest curator, had ever been to New Zealand or seen the objects. Not surprisingly, he was unable to provide much technical information.

Futhermore, the objects selected for *Te Maori* belong to a living culture. The Maori people invest these artifacts with unparalleled significance and spiritual value. This was part of the richness, but it also gave rise to unexpected problems. Every step of the way, Maori beliefs and customs presented a series of high hurdles. In the end, clearing these hurdles contributed to the education and enlightenment of the participants from both sides of the Pacific Ocean.

I drive to work with my colleague and when I get there I am embarrassed because the museum is huge. It is built of massive grey stones and sits alone atop a hill in the park. I realize that my subconscious was expecting a hut.

We are met by a man who has longish grey hair and wears socks with his sandals. He is a curator and has written scholarly books on subjects that interest minute fragments of the world's population. He leads us down a corridor that rings the museum. The corridor is dark and the smells are smells that say nothing has changed here in a century. When we come to a window, what is pretty about Auckland flashes before us.

I stare in wonder as the sea explodes with light and white sails. Then it is gone. We pass green metal cabinets and battered boxes covered with dust. There is another explosion of sea and sails and then the man turns a corner and follows the hallway down a different face of the building. I anticipate the next window but still I am dazzled. On this side Rangitoto Island floats, stark and elegant on a flashing sea. We follow the man through claustrophobic tunnels until he turns again, this time away from the outer corridor to one that cuts deep into the center of the building.

He uses his key to open a small door cut into a bigger one. I am excited now because I am about to see what it is I have come all this way to see. The room is dimly lit and is so small and the ceiling so high that it appears somehow to be a room stood on end. I wait for my eyes to adjust to the dimness.

The room appears to be filled with lumber. Odd-shaped planks lie on the floor and lean against the walls. I am stricken with discouragement, wondering how we are going to work in this place. "I guess you'll need another light," the man says.

I think that we will need a lot more than that. The man goes and when he returns he has a bare bulb on an eight-foot cord. He climbs over some of the lumber to get to a plug. When the glaring light goes on, I see that it is not lumber at all, but some of the artifacts from the exhibition. I am careful not to let my expression change.

I look around now and realize that the things leaning on the wall are also objects for the exhibition. I try to look up, to see the top of them, but the bare bulb has made too much contrast between dark and light. The carvings vanish at about twelve feet, into the shadows. I feel wild, hysterical laughter building up in my throat but I turn calmly to the man and say, "A ladder would be nice." This is a small, silly thing to say but I can think of nothing else. He goes again and when he returns he is carrying a six-foot ladder. I almost look down at the ladder and then up at the carvings, but don't because I feel this would be rude. Instead I smile ambiguously and say thank you. I know that my first day at work has begun.[2]

The difficulties encountered with this exhibition were by no means confined to those stemming from cultural differences. In fact, coordinating the exhibition proved complex from the very beginning. A major loan of ethnographic material from New Zealand was unprecedented; the New Zealand museum community was simply not in the habit of lending its collections. The result: an almost total lack of support systems within the country. This meant that it was hard for the New Zealanders to answer in advance even our basic questions about how to go about doing this project. In turn, the New Zealanders were sometimes frustrated by our approach and by our inability to fully dispel their fears of risk to the objects.

The objects ranged in size from three-quarters of an inch to fifteen feet and in weight from one ounce to a thousand pounds. (The Pukeroa Gateway didn't fit in the elevator at the Metropolitan Museum of Art and it required twenty-eight riggers to haul up the steps.) The objects were nearly all made of wood, bone, or ivory—fragile materials, subject to harm under severe changes in climate. Insurance values ranged widely, from $750 to $5,000,000 but it was clear that no amount of money could make up for any loss or damage to these spiritually laden objects. The psychological pressure was intense.

In late 1982, with loans promised and funding assured, the American conservator and I began to plan our investigatory trip to New Zealand. The purpose of this trip was to determine the ability of the objects to withstand the rigors of international travel; to set the standards of care for the tour; to gather data needed to plan assembly, packing, and transportation; and, concurrently, to amass information required to make application for U.S. government indemnity.

The project was so complex that we were forced to return to basics. It is harder than it sounds to think simply. Registrars, having spent years at this work, have been faced with increasingly complicated exhibitions. Our minds, it seems, jump into high gear as soon as someone waves an exhibition catalogue. We slip all the low gears on the way up. This time, because we knew so little about the exhibition, we had to start at the beginning. This resulted in a valuable by-product: an opportunity to examine the way we think.

What emerged was evidence of a standard, identifiable thought process, a system which, upon examination, reveals three basic elements: brainstorming, the mental dry run, and goal defining. A review of each complex aspect of the exhibition shows that the mental process remained stable, no matter how different the task.

Here is an example: To begin with, how much time would I need to complete this investigatory trip? When I attempted to gauge the amount of time, it became even more obvious how little I knew about the objects, New Zealand, or the overseas museums. My initial mental condition was one of confusion. My mind was filled with a constant stream of seemingly unconnected images: cars, planes, road conditions, copy machines, tripods, screwdrivers. On and on.

In this welter of mind pictures, I groped for a clue that would tell me how long the trip would take. How long? That was it! The answer had to be a number. But I knew that already—wasn't that a meaningless idea? But the thought kept on surfacing. Finally, its importance revealed itself. If the answer had to be a number (How long? Three weeks? Four weeks? Three months?) all the factors leading to the answer must be numbers as well. The trick was to convert all those images bobbing about in the stream of consciousness into numbers: I would have to quantify all those random ideas.

A plan began to emerge. Travel time allocation was easy to compute since it already consisted of numbers of hours and miles. Using a New Zealand road map and some general information on road conditions from a guide book, I could estimate how long it would take to drive between the thirteen cities we knew we must visit. Next, I outlined the standard set of tasks that we would have to accomplish at each location. I knew that we would have to inspect the objects, make condition reports, and photograph the objects to record their condition. The objects would have to be measured, and the records carefully checked to verify that each object was in fact the one requested. I'd have to interview personnel about the availability of temporary packing materials and transportation. There was still no way to determine how long these tasks would take since so many variables were missing. Planning became far more manageable, however, when considered in relation to the objects, of which there were a finite number.

Accordingly, I assigned each object a number based on its size. In this case, size came to represent the amount of time it would take to inspect, photograph, measure, and verify records. The objects fell into four standard size categories, and for each category I estimated handling time—small, fifteen minutes; medium, thirty minutes; large, one hour; extra large, one and one-half hours. It was then possible by simple multiplication to establish how many eight-hour working days we would need at each location.

The trip was beginning to take on quite a definite form. What began as a chaotic stream of confusing thoughts became a simple mathematical equation: land in Auckland on Friday—sleep for two days—handling time for thirty-five objects (mostly large and extra large), five days—finish in Auckland on Friday afternoon—drive to Whakatane Saturday morning (approximately, four hours)—free time until Sunday night—handling time for three objects (small and medium), one-half day—finish in Whakatane by noon Monday—drive to Gisborne Monday afternoon (approximately three hours)—handling time for seven objects (small, medium, and large), one day—finish in Gisborne by Tuesday evening—drive to Napier Wednesday morning . . .

and so on till our return. Map calculations and size-based units of measure indicated that the trip would take six weeks. The calculations eventually proved accurate.

American Federation of Arts
New York, USA

Dear Everyone,

Amazingly enough, the time schedule Cap and I made up in New York based on the numbers of objects and their sizes has worked out. What is a little hair-raising is that we didn't anticipate the ceremonies. They take up a good part of the first day. We spend much of the ceremony and the tea that follows trying not to look at our watches.

Our greeting ceremony in Nelson was like a scene from a Fellini movie. Peta told us to wait by the car; we, the visitors, need to be "called in" by the Maori museum hosts. There was the now familiar off-key wail from the front steps. There was a series of formal speeches in Maori and English. Suddenly a small motorbike appeared, driven by a middle-aged Maori man wearing shorts and one artificial leg. He passed through the narrow space separating our chairs from the speech-making Maoris on the museum steps.

When the speeches were done we were each handed prayer books so we might pray and sing together, thereby becoming one family. The most horrible, unsychronized, gravelly singing imaginable ensued.

Tea was brought out and two bags of chocolate chip cookies were torn open. Suddenly the motorbike appeared from the other side of the building. The one-legged man in shorts looked neither to the right nor the left as he rode through the narrow space separating us from two bags of chocolate chip cookies.

I don't know guys. I just don't know. We're off to Christchurch now.

Love to everyone,
Carol

Some things got left out, but, basically the approach was sound. It turned out that the initial episode of chaotic thought had given rise to a moment of clarity. I understood that the correct way to approach this part of the project was to turn both objects and tasks into numbers, producing numerical answers to my questions. With hindsight, it seemed that the confusion was an important step in reaching that moment of clarity.

This, then, is brainstorming that emerges from the stream of consciousness. It is the first of the three identifiable elements that make up the thought process. This is the time during which it is most important not to edit yourself. Much of the information that drifts through may seem unrelated to the job at hand; in the end some of it will not prove useful. But at an early stage it is impossible to tell what will lead to what so it is a good idea to process freely. This brainstorming, which feels like confusion, is the mind's attempt to bring to the fore everything that will go into a project. It happens naturally. It is not simply confusion or an inability to be focused and directed. In reality, it is a critical element of the thought process, a powerful tool, and something to encourage.

In the case of *Te Maori*, the first brainstorming session produced a variety of images. When the word "screwdriver" surfaced, it was unclear exactly what it had to do with a trip to New Zealand to inspect, measure, and photograph 174 Maori objects. It came up several more times over the next few days. Some attention focused directly on the word screwdriver produced results.

The New Zealanders told us that the museums we were to visit ranged in size and scope from massive war memorials on hill tops to one-room wooden schoolhouses. In some museums, the objects had been stored for decades; in others they were on display. It was likely that some of these objects were undisturbed in display units for more than fifty years. There was the connection! Screwdriver, screws, wood, fasten—the thought that came from the stream of consciousness brainstorming session eventually shed light on what we might find in New Zealand.

It would not be surprising to find ourselves at a museum, working on a tight schedule, only to realize that no one knew how to get into the display case to remove the object. This, in turn, led to another thought. Might we ask museum personnel to locate all the objects and isolate them in one area before our arrival? Here was the beginning of a letter to the thirteen lending institutions.

This is another example of how stream of consciousness brainstorming helped us anticipate working conditions in an unfamiliar setting. The technique proved useful, over and over again. But in the example of the screwdriver, another element in the thought process surfaces—the mental dry run. This begins soon after, or is intermingled with the later stages of brainstorming. The realization that we might arrive at a museum and find ourselves unable to get an object out of its case occurred as a result of mentally picturing that frustrating scene. Using imagery of this kind in a deliberate fashion makes it possible to examine any number of contingencies. Each imagined situation provokes questions and answers. There are few methods as effective for planning.

Using the mental dry run technique, I envisioned myself disembarking from an aircraft at Auckland airport—that is, at my mental version of the airport. Weary and disheveled, I imagine myself claiming baggage, clearing customs and immigration, and leaving the airport. Immediately there is a problem with the script. Am I in a cab? If so, where have I told the driver to go? Here is something I need to find out: Will I go directly to a hotel or do the New Zealanders expect me to meet with them immediately? (Horrors!) And what hotel? Am I to make reservations or will that be taken care of there? Will anyone meet me at the airport? How will I recognize my host? What is the address of the hotel in case I miss my contact? And do I have New Zealand currency to pay the cabby? The more detail in the scene the better. A truly vivid image, crammed full of seeming trivia results in fewer unfortunate surprises. Is it raining when I leave the airport? Pack an umbrella. Is the sun shining? Sunglasses.

Now I go backward for a moment, starting over from the beginning. I had imagined myself claiming baggage. What baggage? Better get that suitcase zipper repaired. How much baggage? I better not over-pack: the imaginary scene shows just how intolerable three suitcases will be after thirty-two hours of travel. And what about clearing immigration? No one on the New Zealand management team has mentioned visas, but that doesn't mean I don't need one: better call the consulate.

The man next to me talks for two hours while I nod and smile. Finally he falls asleep and his neck goes to rubber, his head dipping, occasionally onto my shoulder.

When we get to Auckland it is 6:40 a.m. their time. On a Friday. I think I remember leaving New York on a Monday, but I don't question this. I am very tired.

We are met by a man I have met, thank God, once before in New York. No matter what I do I can't keep my bags from getting between my legs, tripping me. I pray there are no mirrors between here and the car.

"I'll take you to your hotel now so you can freshen up," the man says. "We've scheduled a meeting for noon." "Of course," I say. "That's fine." I spend the rest of the ride thinking how not-fine that is.

I looked a lot more sophisticated in the mental dry run than I did upon arrival in New Zealand, but the reality looked a lot like the dry run. Not that the people, buildings, and landscape physically resembled the mental images, but the work proceeded much as anticipated in the imaginary scenes. There were still surprises, like the bare bulb on a short cord to inspect fifteen foot objects in a dark room with no electrical outlets. Such a problem calls for an on-the-spot solution: no amount of planning can predict it.

I applied the mental dry run technique to the whole trip, right up to my return to the airport. I found it best to do the dry run in stages since marathon episodes lose detail and cause carelessness. I disciplined myself not to leap over any action or event, no matter how insignificant. If in my mind I handed a museum director a copy of a condition report, I asked myself where did I get the copy? Will there be a photocopier in a museum the size of a one-room schoolhouse? Add carbon paper to the list of supplies to take along.

The third identifiable element of the thought process is goal defining. The ultimate goal, in this case, was to produce an exhibition of Maori art that would open at the Metropolitan Museum of Art in September 1984. This was a broad and distant landmark for use only as a directional guide.

It took nine years of preparation to get *Te Maori* to the Metropolitan. In this context, preparation means the setting of intermediate goals—and getting to them. Securing loans and funding, assembling and packing the exhibition, transporting it to this country, planning the opening ceremonies, and a hundred other aspects of the exhibition, served as intermediate goals that shaped and directed the daily tasks. Every once in a while, the project experienced a period when work faltered, as did the sense of direction. These were the times that called for redefinition of goals.

When I returned from New Zealand in 1982, the recognized goal was to make application for U.S. government indemnity by the April deadline. As soon as the Christmas holiday was past, we turned our full attention to this time-consuming and tedious task.

Indemnity requires a detailed account of all aspects of the exhibition with particular attention paid to standards of care, assembly and packing techniques, and transportation methods. Research from the preliminary trip revealed a number of good options—too many, in fact. As a result, it was difficult to establish how to handle the objects from the time they left the lending institutions until they eventually returned to the point of origin. Goal defining was in order.

My first thought was that uncertainty as to who would pack the exhibition hampered completion of the indemnification application. We were prevented from making a decision because we lacked cost comparisons. Bids had not been sought from vendors because specifications had not been drafted. Specifications for what? There was no way to develop "specs" without having a clear sense of crate design. There, at last, was the problem.

When focusing on the immediate deadline for the indemnity application, crate design seemed a vague goal—something in the distant future. Surely the indemnity deadline took priority. Not so. Completion of the application depended on a final plan of action. Therefore, we had to secure the crate estimates, because without them a final plan could not develop. The immediate goal became to design crates.

We attempted to carry the process further, to determine whether anything stood in the way of crate design. We had photographs of every work in the show, along with exact dimensions and estimated weights. We knew individual insurance values, making it possible to group objects so that no one crate carried excessive value. Loan information was on hand making it possible to further spread risk by distributing loans from each collection over a number of crates. Nothing was missing.

Over the next several days, I sorted the data about object size, weight, value, and lender, calculated measurements and determined the necessary allowances for packing materials. Soon, it was possible to mail the approximate inner dimensions for twenty-six crates to three potential builders along with samples of packing materials and photographs of the objects. Now, with crate dimensions in hand, it was also possible to seek costs on ocean freighting the empty crates to New Zealand. (One of the options was to build the crates in New York.)

The process of goal defining, then, is one of working backwards from a larger to a smaller goal. Our grand goal was to open this exhibition at a given site on a specified date. Any project of this magnitude presents obstacles once the work begins. Each obstacle encountered indicates the need for intermediate goal defining. Over time, many, many intermediate goals surface; planners recognize these goals, clarify them, and address the issues that the goals expose.

The preparation of *Te Maori* became increasingly complex during 1983 and 1984. In 1983 came notification that indemnity had been awarded. This lay the groundwork for the exhibition from assembly all the way to return of the works to the lenders in 1986. Indemnity was predicated on approval of the detailed plan in the application. From this point forward the plan could not change without review by the indemnity board. Interestingly, even with no new ground to break, the thought process remained constant. The three basic elements—brainstorming, mental dry run, and goal defining—continued. Now we labored over the same material in a constant attempt to refine and polish the whole.

After receiving the bids for construction of the crates, it was possible to establish a clear, specific plan. A carpenter in Auckland would build the outer crates. In early April 1984, the crates would arrive at the Auckland Museum and the Auckland City Art Gallery, the two consolidation sites for the exhibition.

On April 16, I would arrive in Auckland, make a thorough condition check against the original 1982 reports, and organize the two sites so that packing for overseas transportation could begin. On April 30, our New York art packer would arrive to begin custom-fitting each object to the crate. The New Zealand packer who built the outer crates would assist the New York packer.

At the time this plan sounded splendidly precise and complete. Everything seemed to be in place. Indemnity was no longer in question. On hand was a detailed description of the assembly. We knew what routes we would use in the United States to move the exhibition between venues. We knew what kind of transportation methods we would use, and we had outlined handling specifications. We were all satisfied with a job well done.

In no time at all, and mostly as a result of an attempted mental dry run, the gaps in the plan became obvious. The crates would arrive at the packing sites. But would the empty crates, the objects, the inner packing materials, and a work crew fit into the spaces allocated? Where, actually, was the source of the specified packing material? Was the packer in Auckland to order it? He did not know our interior packing plans. Perhaps the New York packer then? He had never seen the objects! How much foam rubber and flannel did we need to ship to New Zealand? The mental dry run came to an abrupt halt with the empty crates not even in the door of the museum. It was time for another brainstorming session.

Ultimately, of course, these problems were solved. But there were others to resolve when we finally got to Auckland.

"Why," I say, "are sixty people coming to the ceremony? Sixty people will not fit in this tiny room with all these artifacts and all these crates. Can we not use the empty gallery upstairs, that will hold sixty people?"

"The ceremony," he says patiently, "must be held in the room with the objects because the ceremony is to bless the objects."

"Can we not," I say, "take a small selection of the objects upstairs to the empty gallery and let them represent all the objects?" This I say, knowing that it is a bad idea. This I say, knowing that the objects should not be carried upstairs and that there is not enough security upstairs and that there is no climate control upstairs. This I say, also knowing that this man will not budge.

"Done," he says.

"That is fine," I say. "The crew goes home at 4:00 and there will be no one to carry them up after that, so it is important that you be here at 3:00." At 4:15 he is not there and I appoint myself a Maori. I choose this object because it is large, and that one because it is small, those two because they are made of stone and the other because it is whalebone. At 4:45 he is not there and I appoint myself designer. I place that object towards the rear and this towards the front; the other at an angle. I tell the guard he will die a miserable death if he leaves this room even long enough to pee, and I leap in the car.

There is no time for a shower so I wash my face and change into a skirt that has not been properly ironed and I get lost on the way back from my hotel.

The man who was to be there at 3:00 is there. He smiles and kisses me on the cheek. He tells me he has already been in the room and compliments me on what a lovely selection I have made. This is very Maori.

I smile and thank him for the compliment and think that I might just have to kill him. This is very American.

There is no way to cope with on-site crises if the basics haven't been taken care of earlier. Every exhibition planner and registrar knows that crises will happen. Attention to the details of preparation help insure the physical security of the objects and have psychological benefits. The techniques of thinking up solutions to problems—brainstorming, the mental dry run, and goal definition—have staying power, and remain on tap during emergencies. In the end, it comes down to priorities—defining the most important, immediate goal. In the case above, the goal was to make the ceremony happen so we could proceed.

By now it should be clear that the three elements of the thought process are integrated. They function within a related framework and not as separate entities. In effect, the process gives birth to clarity of thought; in turn, this clarity produces the ability to act, the ability to make an idea into a reality. Inevitably, obstacles arise, preventing further movement. There is a halt in the action followed by a session—this can be three seconds or three days long—during which the ideas undergo refinement. Action follows until another obstacle arises: the process starts over.

The three elements repeat again and again: steam of consciousness brainstorming leads to the dry run, which permits clearer definition of goals. Each aspect of the project becomes subject to this repeating pattern of thought, until the whole is laid out, in abundant detail. As planning follows its tortuous path, there is the inevitable reworking of individual tasks. Some things once thought of as centrally important are now relegated to the periphery of the project; other things take on greater weight and urgency. At an advanced planning stage, a mental dry run will meet with few or no obstacles—the end is in sight.

What did I learn from applying this technique to *Te Maori*? The first is that confusion, if allowed to simmer and boil over, will produce the necessary clarity of thought. Also, the mental dry run isn't always totally conscious: it proceeds as the mind is focused elsewhere. The same is true of goal defining. Nevertheless, identifying the process and using the elements deliberately as tools can make any task easier.

Te Maori had a successful U.S. tour: over half a million people saw the exhibition. I doubt that many of these people thought of what went into bringing these treasures to America.

My struggles went on behind the scenes. Yet those struggles are part of the story of *Te Maori*, as exhibition registrars know.

The preparation of *Te Maori* took a long time and demanded a lot—but it gave a lot, too. There was, of course, the personal satisfaction of seeing the exhibition fall into place. On a practical level, the exhibition permitted me to relearn how to think simply and directly about my work—how to use my thought process to tackle the job. This proved to make subsequent tasks smoother and more integrated. Most personally memorable were the magical moments with the Maori people.

It is night time and there is thick fog. I have been up for two days now. I am very tired and try to sleep but the roads are too winding and too slippery, the fog too thick, the cargo too precious.

Close behind us is an unmarked police car with two plainclothes policemen. They too are tense.

Close behind the police car is a mini-bus and a car, filled with elders. I am keenly aware of the bus and the car but pretend that I am not. These are the people about whom I am not supposed to know. "Slow down a little," I say to the driver, "the elders are falling behind."

Now we are coasting off onto a narrow shoulder. "Where are we?" I ask. "Taupiri," he says, "the resting place of the kings." I perch there, wondering how I will explain to the Indemnity Board what we are doing there if something goes wrong. The elders begin, stiffly, to climb out of the bus and the car. It is 2 a.m. I do not want to intrude because I am a foreigner but one of the women comes forward and motions me to climb down. One of the elders calls into the night. He calls to the white grave markers that dot the two hills and the hoarse emotional voice screams into the night fog. Strange feeling begins to crawl in my body and, now, the woman feels me shudder with cold. She opens her coat and wraps me in with her. She is rocking softly back and forth, keening.

A tall, old, old man steps forward. He is bent and stooped but thumps his walking stick with great force on the wet grass. He screams shrilly into the night, waves his stick at the graves and then at the truck waiting by the side of the road. The woman whispers in my ear that these are the graves of the very kings we carry in the truck. She tells me that they are greeting each other and as I look back and forth, from one to the other, my skin prickles with something I cannot name.

127

We climb back into the cars and the truck and the mini-bus. We drive on, and twice more we stop in the night.

Te Maori completed a successful New Zealand tour on September 10, 1987, three years to the day after it opened at the Metropolitan Museum in New York. The artifacts have all been returned to the lending museums.

Carol O'Biso is currently living in New Zealand. Her book, *First Light,* recounting her experiences as the registrar for *Te Maori,* was published in New Zealand in 1987. An American edition is scheduled for 1989. Currently, Carol is writing a screenplay of *First Light.* The film release is expected in 1990.

Notes

[1]The American Federation of Arts organized *Te Maori*, which opened at the Metropolitan Museum of Art, New York, and then continued to the St. Louis Art Museum; the de Young Museum, San Francisco; and the Field Museum of Natural History, Chicago.

[2]Carol O'Biso, *First Light* (New Zealand: Heinemann Publishers, 1987). All extended quotations are from *First Light.*

Accountability

"Let's Kill All the Lawyers": Registrars, Law, and Ethics

JACK FOSS

A few years ago while in Washington to attend the annual meeting of the American Association of Museums, I paid my first visit to the Folger Shakespeare Library. In the shop I circled around a rack of T-shirts imprinted with pithy citations from the plays. The one I was attracted to—but did not buy—would have enabled me to proclaim to the world: "The first thing we do, let's kill all the lawyers." (I may get it on my next visit, and thereafter wear it to certain crucial meetings—like collections management policy drafting sessions.)

The line is from King Henry VI, Part II, and is spoken by Dick the butcher, who is one of the rabble taking part in a short-lived rebellion. Registrars, I decided, would never take part in a rebellion unless it were highly principled and orderly.

And yet who in the museum profession today, faced with the need to comply with statutes and regulations from the federal to the local level on everything from gifts and bequests to handicapped access and endangered species, could not be tempted to give the nod to Dick the butcher's proposal?

Stephen Weil, deputy director of the Hirshhorn Museum and Sculpture Garden, and a lawyer who has written extensively on museum-related legal issues, betrays some sympathy with Dick's impatience when he observes that "the cost of trying to institutionalize goodness may be greater than we realize." Weil goes on to say that he is "no longer as sure as I once was that the lawyers—myself included—are wholly innocent. It is not our intentions that I question, but our proliferation. Lawyers may be likened to nuclear warheads. . . . The endless multiplication of such destructive weapons can have no consequence in the long run but to raise the general level of tension and confrontation."[1]

In later writings Weil does not, to my knowledge, reintroduce the nuclear warhead simile, but takes a more balanced and favorable view of the role he and his colleagues play in museum administration. That this role is a considerable one is undeniable. For as museums have become increasingly complex institutions, they have also become increasingly subject to laws and regulations. Many of the decisions museum administrators make, many of the activities museum staff engage in, have legal implications.

Of course it would be a mistake to throw lawyers at every museum problem or to consult with them before making every museological decision: not everything we do requires professional legal advice. But if consulting with attorneys for every little thing is a mistake, so is *not* consulting with them when they're needed, or worse, relying on the opinions of nonprofessionals. Directors, curators, and registrars must learn to recognize when they are drifting into the amateur practice of law, rein themselves in, and turn to whatever procedure their museum has developed to provide professional legal counsel.

When is it time to call in the lawyers? This isn't always an easy matter to decide. Though it is undoubtedly better to err on the side of caution, overconsultation can be costly and time-consuming. For the museum professional who wants to make an informed decision about when to seek legal advice, resources are available. Some familiarity with precedents and trends is helpful; books and articles, courses and training sessions also provide information on the legal aspects of museum work.

This is particularly important for the registrar since so many of the functions of museum registration impinge on matters of law and professional ethics. These are areas in which the registrar's performance can affect the institution's well-being—from its tax-exempt status to its reputation for integrity with a public grown more perceptive and sophisticated in its demands for accountability.

There is something of the lawyer *manqué* about most museum registrars. It has to do with a penchant for order, for thinking that is at once system- and detail-oriented. Legislators, judges, lawyers, and registrars are professional systematizers, organizers, codifiers, and proceduralists. Although probably sharing the curator's aesthetic or intellectual passion for the museum's collections, the registrar can never permit feeling to eclipse the pragmatic concerns for documentation, legal title, copyright, insurance, and customs—the arduous tallying and listing without which collections would be essentially unmanaged and of limited benefit to the scholars and public.

With the exception of the director, the registrar is a generalist more broadly and intimately involved with collections management and museum operations than other staff professionals. Close to the heartbeat of daily operations, the registrar is often the first to know if institutional policy is working or workable. Whether or not policies and procedures are effective is often the result of the registrar's willingness and ability to be monitor, diplomat, persuader, and—if need be—enforcer. Such experience in the trenches needs to enter into the command-level deliberations that result in institutional planning and policies.

Marie Malaro's seminal article on collections management policies recognizes the close affinity between registrarial thinking and the worlds of law, order, and logical systems. Particularly telling are her deft caricatures of staff and board reactions to "the mere mention of 'collections management.' Curators," she notes, "may stiffen. . . . Trustees often change the subject. . . . Directors may duck. . . . And if registrars smile," she concludes, "they are accused of empire building."[2]

In this era of investigative reporting and increased public attention, museums are learning the wisdom of keeping their own houses in order. It cannot be emphasized too often that every museum, whether an agency of government or privately endowed, is accountable to the public. This accountability has moral and legal dimensions. Most museum income is tax-exempt; and donors of gifts to museums have, until recently, enjoyed sizeable tax advantages. (The 1986 Tax Act dramatically reduced many of the incentives for making charitable deductions, but it is too early to tell what effect this will have on museums.) Museums receive government grants that carry with them requirements for compliance with federal and local statutes and regulations. Museums also routinely encounter international regulations or the laws of foreign countries.

Futhermore, museums and their holdings have increasingly become the focus of public attention. Museums hold mankind's heritage in trust; the public knows this and rightfully demands that this heritage be cared for responsibly. As Feldman and Weil assert, "a new, post-1970 morality has sharpened the public sense that museums cannot be managed as private preserves but must be publicly accountable for the art works they hold in trust."[3] (Of course this is true of museums devoted to other disciplines as well.)

One result of the increased scrutiny has been the development or revision of ethics codes by segments of the museum community. The 1978 AAM report, *Museum Ethics,*[4] is a foundation document that has been followed by codes addressed to the particular ethical and professional concerns of curators (1983), public relations officers (1983), and registrars (1984)[.5] Two other publications that have helped define and set higher standards of staff and institutional performance have been the Association of Art Museum Directors' *Professional Practices in Art Museums* (1971)[6] and Alan and Patricia Ullberg's *Museum Trusteeship,*[7] published by the AAM in 1981.

In addition, many individual institutions have developed and adopted codes of ethical and professional practices for their staff and governing board. Often the development of written policies and codes has been one of the salutary effects of participating (or preparing to participate) in the American Association of Museums' accreditation program.[8]

Another post-1970s phenomenon has been the emergence of fields of endeavor called "museum law" or "art law." Though the exact perimeters of these fields may be imprecise, the questions they address are sometimes all too tangible. Museums have been sued on such matters as authentication, valuation, ownership, acquisitions policies, insurance, copyrights and reproduction rights, royalties, employment practices, hazardous substances, injuries to volunteers, and more. Thus the law student who aspires to the practice of art or museum law needs to become a generalist who can counsel museum clients in their varied activities as employers, importers/exporters, grant recipients, nonprofit corporations, charitable trusts, instrumentalities of government, publishers, restaurant operators, *et cetera*.

Museums are complex organizations subject to a range of statutes and regulations, yet there are few laws that even mention museums. Consequently, since issues may arise from disparate sources, those concerned with protecting the legal interests of museums have found it helpful to look to the legal problems encountered by parallel institutions in the nonprofit and public sectors—universities, hospitals, libraries—for signs of what the legislators and the courts may have in store for us.

Books and articles aimed at educating museum trustees and operating staff on the legal implications of their activities frequently derive their cautionary examples from what Weil has termed "our neighboring archipelagoes" in the nonprofit sector.[9] The Ullbergs, for instance, in their delineation of the trustee's liabilities, cite cases involving a hospital board (nonmanagement and self-dealing) and community college trustees (violation of a faculty member's right to freedom of speech). Referring specifically to the hospital case, they note that "the decision has implications for all nonprofit organizations."[10] We need to put off the blinders that permit us to see only "museum law" or "hospital law" and learn to interpret the extent to which our neighbors' problems may ultimately be our own.

One of the best ways to keep current on the cluster of laws and legal concerns related to museums is to attend the American Law Institute-American Bar Association (ALI-ABA) annual course of study in *Legal Problems of Museum Administration*.[11] Course workbooks and transcripts of sessions have been published yearly since the first seminar in 1973. A glance at the 1987 ALI-ABA program attests to the value of the sessions for registrars and other museum professionals. Among the subjects addressed are bequests to museums, lending across international boundaries, and professional codes of conduct.

The introduction of the ALI-ABA seminars was just one of many events that gradually gave rise to and defined the contours of "museum law." Although early interest in "museum" or "art law" is traceable to the late 1950s, it was not until 1971 that activity in these fields began attracting more visible numbers of groups and individuals. That year marked the publication of *The Visual Artist and the Law* produced jointly by the Associated Councils of the Arts, the Association of the Bar of the City of New York, and Volunteer Lawyers for the Arts. At almost the same time, Stanford University launched a graduate level course—the first of its kind—that dealt with the legal and ethical questions related to the arts. A more dramatic occurrence that year was the suit filed in the California courts by the government of Guatemala against an art dealer, demanding the recovery of stolen property. The dealer had been trying to sell the property to an American museum. Paul Bator notes that it was the "first such suit by a foreign government."[12] Clearly, the field of "art law" was heating up, and museums were in the thick of things.

In 1972 the Practicing Law Institute (PLI) sponsored a workshop in New York entitled *Legal and Business Problems of Artists, Art Galleries and Museums*. Despite certain organizational difficulties, this meeting was valuable in providing a forum for lawyers who had been working individually on art and museum problems. Common interests and broad areas of law impinging on the arts and museums were perceived as needing further exploration.

A spin-off from this workshop (brokered by the Smithsonian Institution) was the first ALI-ABA course of study given at the Freer Gallery in 1973. That same year PLI came back with a second workshop, presented first in New York and then in Los Angeles. One of the basic reference works in the field, Feldman and Weil's *Art Works: Law, Policy, Practice*, published in 1974, was developed from a course handbook for this second Practicing Law Institute workshop.

Publication accelerated during the balance of the 1970s, with many of the volumes authored by lawyers who had participated in the various workshops.[13] As something of a capstone to the decade, Merryman and Elsen's two-volume *Law, Ethics and the Visual Arts* appeared in 1979.[14] Recently, Franklin Feldman and Stephen Weil, with the collaboration of Susan Duke Biederman, have produced *Art Law: Rights and Liabilities of Creators and Collectors*.[15]

A comparable increase in periodical literature occurred in the same time span. *The Hastings Law Journal* and the *Connecticut Law Review* have devoted issues to the problems of nonprofit institutions. *Museum News* reports regularly on legislation affecting museums as well as precedents and trends observable in the outcome of cases. Other specialized periodicals address the points of interaction between law, art, and cultural property, and museums of all disciplines.

Workshops and symposia continue to multiply along with new groups with common interests and agendas. In 1980, for example, the National Association of College and University Attorneys formed a section to deal with the special problems of the university museums.

During the same fifteen-year period, California enacted six laws to protect artists. Most of these laws have at least indirect effects on museums. The California Art Preservation Act of 1980 introduced to the United States the European principle of the moral right (*droit moral*) of the artist in his work. Since *droit moral* involves specific preservation and conservation responsibilities, and even responsibilities that affect exhibition practices, California curators, conservators, and registrars need to be familiar with its provisions.

New York followed California by enacting its Artists' Authorship Rights Act in 1984. Although there are significant differences between the California and New York statutes, it is to be hoped that the example of these two states presages national uniformity in this area of legislation. The lack of such statutes has been termed by John Merryman "an unworthy and intolerable hiatus in our law."[16]

Another California law, effective in 1984, is museum-specific legislation dealing with loans to museums for indefinite or long terms. Its development and adoption in a relatively short span of time was the result of a unique concatenation of people and organizations, prominent among which were the state's registrars.

The legislative project began in September 1982, and nine months later—June 1, 1983—the law was signed by the governor. Two other states, Washington and Maine, had earlier addressed the problem of unclaimed or unidentified objects in the custody of museums and historical societies, and the legislative solutions they reached were starting points for California's approach.

The state's registrars were brought into the act in November 1982, when they received a memo and a ten-page questionnaire from the San Francisco city attorney's office. The purpose of the questionnaire was to provide information needed to draft legislation that would solve the problems and also to collect statistics that would convince the state's lawmakers that a legislative solution was sorely needed.

Drafts of the proposed legislation were circulated to registrars and other interested museum personnel for comment; progress reports were issued; and lists of local legislators were supplied so that registrars could write and call to support the proposed law. Many organizations and individuals contributed to the effective management and success of the project—a professional corporation lobbyist donated services; the Board of Trustees of the Fine Arts Museums of San Francisco authorized staff participation; the state controller offered assistance. But registrars were most prominent on the barricades.

Some of the salient features of the resulting law are (1) a mechanism to terminate loans and to conserve or dispose of loaned property, where necessary, without risk of liability, (2) a means for museums to file notice by publication of their desire to terminate a loan when personal notice is not possible, (3) automatic termination of the lender's rights to loaned property if more than twenty years have elapsed from the date of the last written contact, and (4) protection of lenders and depositors by requiring museums to notify them of the provisions of the law and also of any injury or loss to their property.

The California law is a good model for other states considering a legislative solution to this very common problem, and so too are the tactics and organizational procedures used to bring the project to a successful conclusion. Two key issues warranting the close attention of those who may wish to draft comparable legislation are due process—adequate protection of the right of lenders and depositors—and a reasonable statute of limitations. In addition to requiring twenty-five years of elapsed time without owner contact before the vesting of title in the museum, California has a one-year moratorium from the effective date of notice to the lender until museums can act to terminate owners' rights under this provision. Both the Washington and Maine statutes provide vesting of title in the institution within a shorter period of time (ninety days or sixty days) after the required notice has been sent or published. The California drafters felt that such provisions might be successfully challenged by an owner whose rights were so terminated.

Although registrars did very well as prime movers in a legislative campaign, their basic task is and will continue to be the development and administration of orderly procedures for documenting and managing collections. In discharging this complex responsibility they are in a unique position to further the goals of their institutions, to help establish and protect institutional integrity, and to provide complete, accurate, and timely records. The Ullbergs note that when museums face public inquiry and demands for records and documentation, "the response is often particularly effective when it includes records prepared in the ordinary course of business, for these records are proof that the board routinely discharges its responsibilities."[17]

Whatever sort of architectural front museums may present to their communities and the world, they are all glass houses. They exist for the public to "come and see." The public needs to be able to trust what we show them and what we say about what we show them. These are matters of integrity that begin with candor and honesty from within—with the governing board, the director, and the staff. This sort of climate is fostered by the dialogue that informs the development of codes of ethics and written collections management policies. Registrars should support and actively participate—if not take the lead—in efforts to develop such instruments and keep them alive and working.

The authors of *Museums for a New Century*[18] identify several forces for change that have special bearing on the developing role of the registrar. One of these is the trend towards more democratic, participatory decision-making—a move away from traditional hierarchic structures. Many museums have indeed begun to utilize staff more fully at the policy-making and planning level. This means an expanded role for registrars that will require of them a state-of-the-art awareness of all factors—including the legal—that bear on their responsibilities.

The revolution in communication and information technology is another force for change cited in *Museums for a New Century*. The pace of technological development in communications and information management will not require that registrars become programmers or even that they grow totally comfortable with the inexorable logic of those valuable electronic allies, computers. Registrars will need, however, to develop the ability to communicate to technicians the specifications for systems capable of managing collections data and for converting as many operations as possible to automated modes. The registrar will need to be sensitive to computer security problems and legal requirements for retention of certain data and documents in tangible—that is, hard, as opposed to electronic—form. The ability to keep so much more information about collections in computer memory, and the potential for manipulating and accessing it in countless ways never possible in manual systems, presents an ultimate challenge to anyone charged with orderly and efficient thinking and useful results.

Museums for a New Century also identifies a collaborative spirit that will increasingly unite museums in mutually beneficial projects and shared resources. If this trend towards sharing and cooperation is not to be primarily a reaction to economic exigencies, it must be explored, understood, and adopted for positive, creative purposes. As planners involved in the future of their institutions and as front-line pragmatists who are often the first to learn what works and what does not, registrars will be very effective in developing and participating in cooperative ventures.

The collaborative spirit will also unite museums with other institutions in the nonprofit sector when common problems, such as the need for improved legislation or relief from ill-conceived regulations, can be more effectively addressed and resolved by a coalition of concerned organizations. In these endeavors registrars will be called upon as witnesses, advocates, and lobbyists.

The role of registrars—like that of the institutions they serve—is an evolving one. If the last decade has witnessed augmented respect, and understanding of the registrar, it is because our colleagues have increasingly learned to value registrarial orderliness in an environment that is frequently pressurized and occasionally volatile. As a lawyer has written: "All law resembles art, for the mission of each is to impose a measure of order on the disorder of experience without stifling the underlying diversity, spontaneity, and disarray."[19]

Notes

[1]Stephen E. Weil, *Beauty and the Beasts: On Museums, Art, the Law and the Market* (Washington, D.C.: Smithsonian Institution Press, 1983), 131.

[2]Marie C. Malaro, "Collections Management Policies," *Museum News* 58, no. 2 (November/December 1979): 57.

[3]Franklin Feldman and Stephen E. Weil, *Art Works: Law, Policy, Practice* (New York: Practicing Law Institute, 1974), v.

[4]American Association of Museums, *Museum Ethics* (Washington, D.C.: American Association of Museums, 1978).

[5]*Museum News*, February 1983, October 1974, and February 1985, respectively, for the texts of the curatorial, public relations and registrar codes.

[6]Association of Art Museum Directors, *Professional Practices in Art Museums* (Savannah: The Association of Art Museum Directors, 1971).

[7]Alan D. Ullberg and Patricia Ullberg, *Museum Trusteeship* (Washington, D.C.: American Association of Museums, 1981).

[8]Patricia E. Williams, "The Value of Accreditation," *Museum News* 62, no. 6 (August, 1984): 55–8.

[9]Weil, *Beauty and the Beasts*, 104.

[10]Ullberg and Ullberg, *Museum Trusteeship*, 88.

[11]American Law Institute/American Bar Association, *Legal Problems of Museum Administration*, course of study workbooks and transcripts (Winston-Salem: ALA-ABA, published annually since 1973).

[12]Paul M. Bator, *The International Trade in Art* (Chicago: University of Chicago Press, 1981), 70.

[13]For a more detailed discussion of the earlier evolution of art law, see Stephen E. Weil, "Some Thoughts on 'Art Law,'" *Dickinson Law Review*, 85, no. 4 (Summer 1981), reprinted in Weil, *Beauty and the Beasts*, 199–209.

[14]John Henry Merryman and Albert E. Elsen, *Law, Ethics and the Visual Arts: Cases and Materials*, 2 vols. (New York: Mathew Bender, 1979).

[15]Franklin Feldman, Stephen E. Weil, Susan Duke Biederman, *Art Law: Rights and Liabilities of Creators and Collectors*, 2 vols. (Boston: Little, Brown and Company, 1986).

[16]J.H. Merryman, quoted by Weil, *Beauty and the Beasts*, 228.

[17]Ullberg and Ullberg, *Trusteeship*, 71.

[18]The Commission on Museums for a New Century, *Museums for a New Century*, (Washington, D.C.: American Association of Museums, 1984).

[19]Paul A. Freund, quoted in John Henry Merryman and Albert E. Elsen, *Law, Ethics and the Visual Arts* (New York: Mathew Bender, 1979), viii.

The Essential Collections Inventory

PEGGY SMITH FINCH

*Y*ou're standing in the storage
room, clipboard in hand. Attached to the clipboard is the latest list of
what ought to be on shelf twenty-two. Now is the moment of reckoning.

The shelf is burdened with objects awaiting examination. You
remember the four brass candlesticks from an exhibition of Victoriana
a few years ago. Are they listed? Yes, they are: AH 1978.2345 through
2348. Good! Shelved beside the candlesticks are candle snuffers—one
is silver, and the other has a silver head and a walnut handle. Both
are in very good condition. The record keeping, however, is not.

The snuffers are numbered—thank heavens for that—but the numbers don't appear on the list. Were the candle snuffers mis-shelved? Or
never entered into the record? You'll have to track the history of the
candle snuffers to find out where they belong—and possibly to whom.
What if they were loan items accidently shelved here and never returned?
A number of dreadful possibilities loom in your mind.

You make an appropriate notation about the snuffers on your list,
and hoping you've seen the worst of today's problems, you move on
to the next object. It looks like a dinner bell from the 1920s. But there
is no number at all on the bell; what's more, the clapper is damaged.
And no dinner bell appears on the shelf list. The palms of your hands
begin to perspire; the back of your neck feels clammy. You glance at
your list and notice four more items—a set of Victorian oyster forks
and three engraved matching napkin rings. You remember the donation.
The oyster forks and napkin rings were used by President Garfield.
You look back at the shelf. No oyster forks, no napkin rings. They
are not on the shelf. They are not on the shelf! *Everything begins
to swim before your eyes; your throat constricts; anxiety envelops you
like a mist. Suddenly, you wake up shaking, tangled in the sheets.*

Could this happen? Could this happen today? Of course, for today is inventory day at your museum.

An inventory in disarray is a registrar's nightmare. When information, which should invariably flow through prescribed channels, is somehow diverted or lost, it demonstrates that the museum cannot keep track of the objects in its collections. It may also indicate something worse—for inventories have a way of spotlighting problems with uncanny accuracy, revealing abuses that some would prefer remain hidden.

On the other hand, an inventory that reveals few discrepancies between the written record and what's on the shelf is something a museum can point to with pride, a key indicator of sound collections management.

The Inventory Defined

The museum profession defines the word "inventory" in a number of ways. Inventory refers to the actual holdings of a museum; more narrowly, it refers to the manual or automated records that document these holdings. Inventory is also used as a verb, meaning the activity of accounting for the objects in a collection, whether by creating records or reviewing them for accuracy. All museums need to *inventory* collections; an accurate *inventory* is essential for the museum to fulfill legal and ethical obligations.

Regardless of volume or variety, the value of a museum's collection depends on the well-being of individual objects or artifacts. Basic to collections care is proper documentation of each object's current status, condition, and location. The essential inventory allows the museum to track, examine, evaluate, and subsequently provide appropriate treatment for every object in its custody.

Museums differ in operation, statement of purpose, general audience, and type of artifacts collected. Nevertheless, all museums are in the business of protecting and preserving objects. Many museums receive public money, and enjoy nonprofit tax status. Thus museums are accountable to the public for the careful handling of collections. An inventory is a fundamental part of this collections management, and is crucial to maintaining accountability.

Museums wish to avoid entanglement with the state attorney general's office, the Internal Revenue Service, and government agencies entrusted with protecting the public's interests. To legal watchdogs, a collection of objects differs little from a bank account held in trust for the citizens—consequently, the uses of museum collections are limited by statute to activities directly related to the organization's nonprofit purposes. This normally includes study, display, and preservation for the public's education, entertainment, and welfare. An inventory is a way to guarantee that the collection is available for these purposes.

Failure to account for the location, the condition, or the value of an artifact is an invitation to investigation and, in the most flagrant examples of trust violation, prosecution. Various government agents may request to view (for example) donated materials and supporting documentation. Sloppy or incomplete records make skeptics of federal, state, or local authorities. They know that poorly maintained records foster loss, deterioration, and other abuses. Conversely, a museum that produces complete, accurate, and up to date records, created in the normal course of business, is well prepared for even rigorous probing.

Museums must also answer directly to the public. When Mrs. Smith wishes to see her aunt Thelma's tea service, donated in 1950, it is important to locate it quickly. If it can't be found, the museum's reputation suffers, further donations by the Smith family can be ruled out, and a visit from the attorney general's office may be imminent. Incidents of this sort tarnish the image of the entire profession, and endanger the special considerations museums currently enjoy.

Other museum users include the scientific and scholarly communities, for whom museums serve as repositories and caretakers of objects, artifacts, and specimens. These collection items must be kept in good condition and be readily available for study and examination.

To accommodate its many users, and to assure adherence to the law, a museum must maintain an effective inventory. Records must facilitate comparison between an object and its documentation. The creation of an inventory record for each and every object is one solution.

An inventory record should be concise. It might include the following information:

- accession or loan number
- object name
- condition notation
- permanent storage location
- sublocation (for exhibition or loan)
- size or space requirement for storage

These are the fewest categories of data needed to document, locate, and determine the condition and physical safety of an object in the museum's collection. At inventory time, however, everyone involved with the collection lobbies for additional categories. The curator requests a category for objects that bear dates or maker's marks; the conservator pleads for material of manufacture. Another colleague makes a case for method of acquisition, insurance value, and donor restrictions—all important, useful categories of information. Circumstances may warrant additional categories, but proliferation of categories will increase the time it takes to complete the inventory.

The inventory record is a basic tool whose purpose is to account for, and locate, objects in the collection. While the information in the inventory record appears in the catalogue record, the latter is denser. Museum catalogues list subject, provenance, historic associations, manufacturing techniques and materials, artist and maker, and any number of other classifications. Cataloguing favors lengthy descriptions, notes about exhibitions and publications, and conservation histories. Such information is vital to the complete documentation of the object, but delays inventory efforts.

To perform an inventory a museum needs not only well-maintained records, but well-organized storage areas. Unfortunately, many museum storage facilities are overcrowded. Yet even with adequate storage space, collections may be idiosyncratically organized, defying logical classification and retrieval. Here, natural science museums enjoy an advantage since their specimens are stored according to taxonomic groupings. History and art museums do not enjoy a comparable, established standard. At best, their storage design reflects the environmental needs of objects or the research goals of the institution; at worst, the storage plan is the result of habit and no longer serves needs or goals. Numeric equivalents for storage locations become mandatory—rows of drawers, shelves, racks, and cabinets receive sequential numbers.

Numeric equivalents for storage and gallery locations promote precise recording. In turn, precise recording allows efficient review of all objects assigned to a particular location (e.g., Fish Division, tank seven) or to a range of locations (e.g., area Y, row two, shelves one through six). For example, a person seeking brass candlesticks numbers 86.10.1 & .2 would refer to the code that indicates the exact shelf location, eliminating the need to search through an entire section of candlesticks.

Whether storage is taxonomic or numeric, an orderly record of objects, as stored, facilitates inventory. Automated records can be printed in this order; cards of manual systems can be kept in location order. A person doing an inventory need only move from shelf to shelf, row to row, checking artifacts against the record. Readily available inventory records, in location order, provide the staff with simple comparative information.

An inventory not only assures accountability, but contributes to the care and conservation of objects. Condition, best expressed by a code or abbreviation, is vital to the inventory record. Inventory staff, while not usually conservators, can identify the objects in greatest need of attention. This information, passed on to the conservation staff, results in conservation planning and eventual object treatment. Thus an inventory serves as a rudimentary, but clearly important, conservation survey.

An accurate inventory is integral to the physical security of objects and permits staff to undertake regular location reviews, identify losses, and initiate the search for missing objects. The sooner an object is known to be missing, the greater the chance of return. Spot-check inventories are also helpful in containing losses. It's smart to conduct spot-checks of high-risk collections such as gems or weapons, and to lavish attention on public areas and study collections that are in high demand.

In the event of catastrophic loss involving entire galleries or storage areas, the well-maintained inventory enables rapid identification of all materials stored in the affected areas. Any such museum disaster necessitates reference to inventory records, which themselves need protection. Prudence dictates that a duplicate copy of inventory records be maintained in a safe location, preferably off-site.

Getting to an Inventory

Collections staff may find it difficult to gain support from trustees and directors for inventory projects. Typically, inventories reveal inadequacies; directors and trustees are understandably apprehensive about uncovering touchy legal or ethical issues, or problems that are expensive to solve. To convince management of the value of exposing loss, or revealing conservation needs or deficient collections care, requires diplomacy, sound reasoning, and persistence. Ultimately, directors recognize the wisdom of internal review; better to address weaknesses with a measured plan of action than to have problems uncovered by the attorney general, a donor, or a reporter.

Curators, too, worry about the impact of an inventory. They fear that an inventory may diminish their control over collections or that it may encourage more access to the collections than they personally desire. Curators can be convinced that inventory data enhance research and exhibition opportunities by clarifying holdings; in addition, an inventory is likely to result in improved collections care.

If the first barrier to an inventory is the reluctance of trustees, directors, and curators, the second is the disorganized storage area. Chaotic storage conditions make even the stout-hearted turn back. Sometimes, the full extent of the problem is not apparent until the inventory is under way. Consequently, initial inventories often include a reorganization of storage areas to make the collections more accessible.

Inadequate storage may make desperately needed reorganization seem impossible. Nevertheless, it is important to inventory collections even under deplorable conditions. Dim, unheated warehouses, decades of dust, and poor air circulation are all conditions inventory managers endure. Furthermore, they become expert at devising impromptu solutions. If part of the collection is stored in shoe boxes stacked to the ceiling, one solution is to number the boxes and record them as storage locations. If baskets are stacked one within another, each will be carefully recorded by row, unit, and shelf, and each will be stored as safely as possible under the circumstances.

The third barrier on the way to an inventory is funding. Inventory lacks the fundable romance of an exhibition or the appealing mystery of conservation. An inventory calls for additional supplies and personnel; and, if the museum wishes to automate record keeping, hardware and software costs become factors.

Inventory requires the support of top management, an adequate financial base, and the dedication of the staff that will carry out the work. Usually, the registrar has primary responsibility for planning, managing, and maintaining the inventory. To the registrar's expertise in records management the curator and the conservator will add their skills. A level-headed conservator plays an indispensable role when the inventory uncovers deteriorating or damaged artifacts. Curators will verify data and establish standard terminology.

Strict definitions and consistent usage are key to the efficiency of the recording method. An inventory manual that defines information standards will help assure consistency. The manual should list abbreviations that substitute for descriptive information. These abbreviations serve as pointers to conservation reports and catalogue records. For example, a condition rating may be a number from one through five. Such simple codes are easily transferred from a manual to an automated system.

When inventory begins, it always involves physical inspection of the objects. Inventory personnel need training on how to handle works of art, valuable objects, and delicate specimens. They must also be able to identify conservation problems.

Either museum staff or trained volunteers may serve as inventory personnel. Properly trained volunteers will know when to call upon the curator, conservator, or registrar. With training, a readable manual, and sound direction and supervision from the inventory manager, volunteers can produce accurate, high-quality inventories.

Doing the Inventory

Your trustees and director are behind you. There's money in the budget. The conservator and the curator are eager to help. Volunteers are at the ready, manuals in hand, and museum staff are prepared to direct and supervise. What happens?

The shelf inspection. Real people enter a real museum storage area (or possibly a display area) and examine the contents. The inventory specialist records the number of the object and its location. The object may get some basic attention. The bronze ewer may be dusted; Cambodian silks will be refolded; fresh chemicals will be added to jars of fish specimens.

The shelf inspection provides an opportunity to address problems of physical care. Objects in urgent need of conservation stand out. The inventory specialist, poised to record the condition of the object lying in the drawer, finds a nineteenth-century print, wrapped in a crumbling, yellowed sheet of paper. The specialist removes the shreds of paper and replaces them with inert material; the curator of prints is alerted that something of interest languishes in area B, drawer seventeen.

Objects found during the inventory may present hair-raising difficulties. Some have illegible or obliterated numbers or no markings at all. Others are not where expected; worse, they are missing. Yet other items are discovered in wretched condition, or seem totally inappropriate to the museum's collection, candidates for deaccessioning.

As in the registrar's nightmare, inventory reveals discrepancies between what's on the shelf and what's in the records. The process of resolving those discrepancies is called *reconciliation*. Inventory personnel compare shelf data to previously existing records. Where the records do not match, they must be reconciled. This entails research and investigation.

Many difficulties arise at reconciliation, some with legal implications. For example, the inventory will reveal items *without* records—that is, objects whose accession status is unknown. The collections management policies of many museums include procedures to accession these materials so the museum can take formal responsibility for them. It is important to document the materials as well as the museum's diligent efforts to uncover information about them, as this may affect the museum's right to clear title.

An inventory may also turn up the enigmatic "permanent loan." In the past, museums routinely borrowed material without review procedures. The owners died or moved, and the museum did little or nothing to resolve the status of the material. In effect, the material was abandoned. Other objects are classified as permanent loans when the inventory reveals that their documentation is incomplete: an unsigned gift transaction, for example, would so affect the object's status. The museum's options vis-à-vis permanent loans are severely limited. A museum cannot even conserve the object without the owner's consent, even if its condition is unsound.

For still more agony, the inventory and subsequent reconciliation may reveal materials taken illegally from the country of origin or taken in violation of international regulations. Human remains and objects that have spiritual significance raise yet other questions, and require sensitive handling and extraordinary treatment.

It is the job of the inventory manager to inform the director, curator, and other colleagues of the problems and successes for the inventory project. Whereas some dilemmas require in-depth legal analysis (and will be referred to legal counsel) others can be addressed in the museum's collections management policy.

A comprehensive policy is of inestimable value to the museum grappling with thorny issues. In addition to defining materials appropriate to the museum's collections, the policy should contain answers to questions about deaccessioning or how to deal with objects in poor condition. The policy should also make recommendations regarding permanent loans, abandoned property, and materials from unknown sources. In anticipation of these difficulties, it is a good idea to review and update the collections management policy prior to inventory.

Once an inventory is compiled, its management and maintenance rests with the registrar. Maintenance includes the timely entry of location changes and the prompt addition of new accessions. The registrar maintains data consistency, gains consensus for new terms, and insures data integrity. In addition, maintaining a current inventory includes random spot checks and planned, cyclical inventories.

Inventory is a perpetual phenomenon. An inventory plan—a document that describes who will inventory what, when, and how often—is an invaluable tool. Not only are objects and specimens constantly on the move—from conservation lab to exhibition area to storage to another museum as a loan—but objects are constantly entering the museum. Since comparatively few objects are deaccessioned, the inventory is always growing, always in flux.

Furthermore, some objects—those on exhibit or those of high monetary value—require almost continual inventory: locations may be checked daily, hourly, or even more frequently. Routine assignments, conducted faithfully, insure secure collections. Guards may be responsible for counting the paintings on the wall or the objects in a exhibit case; a staff member may do an hourly check of a world-famous diamond. The best security is to integrate inventory procedures into the normal course of business.

Three Real-Life Examples

In real life, museums sometimes initiate inventories; at other times, outside forces compel the museum to start formal accounting of its collections. At the Smithsonian Institution, the "Great Count" began at the request of Congress; at the Museum of the American Indian, the state attorney general demanded a tally; the Children's Museum of Indianapolis conducted an inventory as the museum began to automate.

The inventory project at the Children's Museum in Indianapolis had tremendous support from museum trustees, upper-level management, and curatorial staff. A complete inventory had not been done since the museum moved into a new building in 1976; prior to the inventory, collection control rested with the curators; the registrar managed entry and exit records.

As part of a larger project to automate collections management functions using the museum's computer, the Children's Museum staff desired to establish accountability but realized that data entry for complete catalogue records would take too much time. It seemed smarter to do a physical inventory of the collections, capturing "accountability factors": accession number, classification, object name, condition, method of acquisition, location, sublocation, date of inventory, and source (donor, lender, or vendor).

Source was included as an inventory field because the registrar had long suspected that there were large holes in the donor and vendor cross reference files. Under these conditions, donor inquiries probably presented the greatest risk of exposing collections management weaknesses. Such exposure could have harmed the museum's relations with its public, deterred potential donors, and jeopardized the museum's nonprofit status. The inventory provided the first major opportunity to review donor records against actual holdings. In order to make the inventory more useful to curators, such fields as country of origin, material, and technique of manufacture were also added.

After the compilation of inventory information from objects in the collections storage areas, catalogue data was added from the museum's manual records. This allowed a cross-check between objects and records.

The museum now supports a collections manager who maintains the collection information database. It is an easy matter to produce inventory records in location order for cyclical inventory review and spot-checks.

The Museum of the American Indian inventory resulted from complaints of mismanagement to the state's attorney general. The museum was required to provide a full accounting of collection material. A team of museum staff began by entering data from the manual catalogue system into a computer. A second team began the physical inventory of storage and exhibition areas. The reconciliation or cross-check yielded a list of missing objects. An added benefit of this inventory was a much needed reorganization of storage.

The attorney general's action dramatizes the importance of regular inventories as a basic precaution against misuse of the collections. In the eyes of the attorney general an accurate inventory was the best method of documenting the museum's objects and activities involving those objects.

At the Smithsonian Institution, the inventory began when Congress requested an accounting of the Smithsonian's holdings and provided funds for this gargantuan project. Because different units within the Smithsonian had different objectives, the inventory program was tailored to the specific needs of each unit. In the department of anthropology, for example, the objectives included location control over the nearly two million specimens in storage, a condition report for every object, and an estimate of storage requirements. One of the uses of the data would be to help in the planning of the new Museum Support Center, the future home of the collection.

In many units of the Smithsonian, staff simply could no longer perform a physical inventory with manual records; they were overwhelmed by wall-size banks of catalogue cards. The solution was to hire data-entry specialists to enter certain catalogue data into a computer while museum staff examined and recorded the objects and specimens. A comparison of the two records revealed discrepancies, which were then reconciled. In other units, staff took existing computer print-outs of collections records into the storage areas, to compare them directly with the objects.

Smithsonian inventory practice specifies two levels of control: "object" level and "lot" or "collection" level. "Object" level materials represent individual specimens of intrinsic or scientific value that are tracked as single items. "Lot" or "collection" level control is for materials that occur in large groups or batches, where the batches are considered as single entities. Examples include mounted insects, potsherds, and plant specimens. Material controlled at the "lot" level is eventually broken down and specimens tracked and treated individually. Refining inventory data enhances intellectual meaning; the data become useful to the research goals of the unit.

In Conclusion

What can be learned from these examples? One lesson is that legal intervention should not be necessary to enforce a museum's stewardship over its collections. Regular inventories help prevent abuses and carelessness, and result in more conscientious attention to the collections. Another lesson is that inventories are not painless; they require resources, attention to detail, and cooperation between staff and between departments. Finally, inventories uncover problems, yes, but they help solve them, too; once problems are identified, staff can shape solutions that result in improved collections care.

The inventory record is basic to sound museum management: it embodies the information needed for minimum collections accountability. The professional code of ethics for registrars states that collections records should be "complete, honest, orderly, retrievable, and current." This is the essence of effective collections inventory, without which collections may suffer abuse, loss, and deterioration. Minimizing risks should override concerns about problems uncovered by inventories. It is the registrar's task to understand the importance of the essential collections inventory, to convince colleagues and management of its value, and to insure that the inventory is an effective collections management tool.

Risk With Good Reason

BILL ALLEN

In a small art museum, a hurried meeting is called in the director's office. The local weather report has announced a tornado watch. If the twister hits, the main gallery's plate glass windows may buckle or shatter. "Do we have enough plywood in storage to board up the windows?" someone asks. "Even if we had the plywood, there's not enough staff here to do the job," says the director.

During a black tie reception, a janitor employed by a cleaning service steals some Renaissance jewelry from a display case. The police apprehend the thief, but the jewelry has been melted down. The cleaning service does not have adequate insurance and files for bankruptcy to avoid the claim. The museum's insurer pays the loss, but cannot recover from the cleaning company. The museum's premium rises astronomically.

At the airport in New Delhi, an American registrar and several Indian officials watch as handlers remove cargo from the plane. After several years, precious artifacts are returning to their mother country. Seventeen crates are out; there's only one more to go. But crate eighteen never emerges. Despite tight security, the crate seems to have disappeared during the stopover in London.

Fact or fiction? Alas, some of the worst museum horror stories are not the product of an over-heated imagination. They've actually happened. That's why risk management is basic to the health of the museum. You simply cannot do without it.

Who does the risk management in your museum? Most other

businesses—and make no mistake that running a museum is a business—designate a single person as "risk manager." In museums, that duty often falls to several individuals who, in their particular areas of responsibility, must answer the question: "What would happen if . . .?" This fragmented approach to risk management is in itself hazardous. All the more reason why museums must be well prepared for emergencies, and adopt a unified plan of action.

Risk management is not about finding set solutions to a series of problems. If this were so, the risk manager could rest easy after identifying the solutions. Unfortunately, events move too swiftly for that; and even organizations that protect themselves from loss or damage may experience an unpredictable catastrophe. No risk management plan can include every possible contingency, but a staff that has practiced risk management is better able to cope with the unexpected. Risk management is therefore an ongoing strategy that requires constant attention.

In a museum, whoever is responsible for minimizing the risk of loss or damage to collections must meet regularly with those responsible for building maintenance and security. The policy makers for the museum—trustees, director, business manager—must also take part in emergency planning and in formulating the risk management strategy. The participation of officers and trustees helps assure adequate funding for risk management. Working together increases the likelihood of identifying all potential risks. It enables the museum to develop realistic policies and procedures to control both the chance and the extent of possible loss.

Museums are susceptible to both "inside" and "outside" perils. "Inside" dangers emanate from the state of the building or physical plant, from employee practices or employee dishonesty, or from inadequate security. The "outside" risks include theft (by persons not associated with the museum) and natural disasters. Some losses or damage to collections will result from a combination of both. The museum's risk management strategy rests on the correct identification of all such perils.

Preparing for the Worst

Natural disasters are the least likely cause of loss or damage. But when they do occur, the results can be devastating. A good way to prepare for such eventualities is to rehearse disaster scenarios. What might happen to the museum building, to collections, to staff, during a fire? A flood? A windstorm? Risk managers, together with department heads, must assess the museum's needs in any perilous situation and develop a formal approach to the unexpected.

Improvising solutions in the middle of an emergency is usually ineffective, and may not even be possible. Disasters typically call for intensified staff support but only properly trained staff will know what is expected of them. A museum that does not prepare its staff may pay a high price. Untrained staff will make mistakes, get in the way, panic, or disappear. If the emergency affects the whole locale—as would an earthquake—staff will consider the safety of their families and homes before the safety of the museum.

Upon whom can a museum depend in the midst of chaos? A disaster preparedness plan allows risk managers to identify the museum's needs, locate outside resources if necessary, and train staff—before the emergency occurs.

Day to Day Loss

Disaster scenarios familiarize staff with the possibilities of loss from extraordinary events; identifying day to day possibilities of loss reaps even greater rewards. For example, if the people who pack and ship collections objects are incompetent, repeated losses will occur. If collections management systems are cumbersome, staff will circumvent them, thus inviting a breach in security.

Scrupulous personnel hiring practices are among the most effective ways of preventing loss and damage. Checking background and personal references will do much to curtail hazards. Competent, well-trained, and equitably paid staff will develop

163

and maintain systems to protect museum property.

Exposure to risk often comes not from the museum's own employees but from contracted suppliers of goods and services. Such outside suppliers should be checked out too: if loss should occur, is the supplier's insurance adequate? Are the outside employees properly trained? Are they honest and reliable?

A salutary exercise for a museum risk manager is to take a walk through the museum, both the public and private space, and evaluate it from the perspective of a thief. Where are the areas of vulnerability? How easy is it for someone to enter supposedly secure areas? Are there times of the day when this is easy to do? Are there objects of high value stored or displayed in unsupervised areas?

The Low-Risk Museum

No matter the condition of the physical plant, examining risk scenarios will yield valuable insights. Many museums occupy buildings never meant to be repositories of precious objects, or that were designed long ago for less perilous times. All the more reason to scrutinize the building and the collection practices. Do exhibitions create blind spots that hinder security? Are values distributed so that loss to a single area will not have a catastrophic effect on the museum? Are storage vaults below ground level subject to flooding? Are collections stored in an attic whose roof may leak? These are some of the many questions that the occupants of any museum building should ask.

Sometimes museum administrators do not realize that there is free or low-cost expertise on hand to help secure the premises and collections. Upon request, most museum insurers will provide a free inspection that can uncover hidden weaknesses. The local fire department, another important ally, can identify fire hazards. Risk managers should take the time to familiarize fire fighters with the museum as a physical plant and solicit their suggestions. Fire fighters will work with museum managers to protect community treasures and high-value collections.

In addition, some communities have agencies that are expert in containing flood or earthquake damage. Local colleges and universities sometimes have engineers or other professionals who are knowledgeable about damage control. For small museums that cannot afford expensive consultants, these are welcome resources.

The best time to take risk-control measures is before a building is built. The fortunate few whose institutions are about to embark on new construction—a completely new museum, a new wing, or renovation—have a chance to improve on the status quo. Architects are not museum professionals and cannot be expected to see the risks as staff do.

Registrars can contribute greatly to building a low-risk museum. As a member of the team that meets with the architects, the registrar's knowledge of collections management systems can uncover potential risk. For instance, the registrar can describe the hazards of receiving collections, gift shop inventories, and restaurant supplies at the same dock. The registrar will also know how new acquisitions move through the building—from holding and isolation areas to conservation, from photography and specimen preparation labs to cataloguing and storage areas, all the way to exhibition facilities.

The registrar has an overview of the museum, and understands the need for access to collections as well as the complexities of collections security. An item in the collection may present many different kinds of risk exposure and must be protected from all; yet the item must remain accessible. An important archival document may be susceptible to insect infestation and, because it is signed by a famous person, may also be a target for thieves. The museum must guard against these perils without totally isolating the document. Weapons, gems, human remains, medical collections, politically sensitive materials, all have risk potential for different reasons. The registrar, responsible for finding safe havens for each collections type, can focus and balance the sometimes conflicting needs. The registrar, in collaboration with other professional staff members, can plan an environment that is both tailored to staff work habits and has low risk potential. For example, many museum programs depend on significant numbers of volunteer staff. How does a museum make effective use of part-time staff while protecting the collections from unnecessary handling?

The location of the registration unit also influences the security of collections. If the registrar's office is too far removed from collection vaults, packing, shipping, and receiving, supervisory functions become difficult to maintain. The registrar's contribution to the development of the physical plant heightens the effectiveness of the collections management program.

Self-Insurance

Some museums insure their permanent collections; others insure only those objects borrowed or loaned. A museum that insures only what it borrows or lends is self-insured for any loss to the permanent collection. Such a museum does not share this part of the risk of loss with any other party. Many museums are partially self-insured. Their insurance covers a percentage of the collection value; the rest is self-insured.

Museum managers may choose to spend their limited funds on security rather than on insurance premiums. Dollars may be directed to inventory control programs, personnel selection and training, or electronic monitors. The principle these museums follow is that enhancing museum skills and operations can reduce risk to an acceptable level.

The museum director and the board of trustees have a fiduciary responsibility to the museum and to the public. They are bound by law to a "standard of reasonable care," also called the "prudent man rule." This means that they must exercise that degree of care, skill, and diligence in their professional practices that a reasonable professional—or a "prudent" man or woman—in the same time, place, and circumstances would have exercised. If loss occurs, the courts could decide that the risk management efforts of director and trustees did not meet the "standard of reasonable care," and that they are therefore personally liable.

Establishing a reasonable limit of liability—how much risk to insure, how much risk to assume—can be a complex undertaking. Collections values usually far outstrip the museum's financial ability to provide a risk-free environment. Reliable data for collections holdings may not exist. A realistic appraisal of the collection at current market value may be more than staff or trustees can accomplish. Even identifying the one hundred most important collection pieces or the 10 percent of the collection at greatest risk may require leadership on the part of the registrar.

Sharing the Risk

There are many ways in which a museum can share the risk for collections or borrowed objects. The lender may agree that the borrower does not have to insure the object at all. Or the lender and borrower may agree to let a third party maintain insurance or security for the object. Loan agreements spell out exactly what kind of coverage the borrower is to provide and what perils the lender self-insures. Loan agreements are legally binding, and may or may not be backed up by an insurance contract.

Museums sometimes make agreements that go beyond the scope of their insurance coverage. For example, a collector may be willing to lend an object to a museum if, and only if, the object is covered against damage caused by vermin. Since most museum insurance contracts routinely exclude such damage, the museum would have to execute a special loan agreement. In effect, the museum self-insures for this contingency.

Insurance is the most common way of sharing the risk. In reality, insurance is a form of gambling. The insurance company takes a bet—the premium—that the museum's paintings will not be stolen, that the political posters will not be vandalized, that the fragile tribal masks will survive transit undamaged.

Besides taking on part of the museum's risk, and settling any resultant claims, the insurance company provides another benefit. Before the company accepts the "bet" it will inspect the museum in order to verify the adequacy of risk management efforts. In this way, the company contributes to the museum's risk management program.

The insurance company may insist on a number of improvements. An emergency exit too near an exhibit case may require a time-delay lock to give guards enough time to foil a thief. The museum may have to connect its intrusion detectors, and fire and smoke alarms, to a central station alarm switchboard. Motion detectors may have to be installed wherever high-value items are stored or exhibited. The inspection lets the museum know what the insurance company considers an acceptable risk. But the museum's standards should in fact be higher than those demanded by the insurer.

Not every museum can obtain insurance. Small museums, for example, seldom have the resources to install sophisticated security systems or to provide guards twenty-four hours a day. If not convinced of the museum's ability to manage risk, the insurance company may be unwilling to "take the bet." If it does, it will limit coverage—that is, hedge its bet by requiring the museum to retain part of the exposure. A company may offer "named perils" coverage instead of "all-risk," or exclude coverage of breakage or dishonest acts of employees, or require a very high deductible.

The most important thing the registrar of a small museum can do is focus staff attention on maintaining the highest possible security standards. Accurate, complete, and timely records are the foundation of museum security. Only by demonstrating its commitment to security will the museum have a choice of insurers or policies.

Art museums frequently demonstrate high standards of risk management. The collections are usually smaller than those of history and natural history museums and therefore easier to control. Art is usually very valuable and highly portable. Premiums are comparatively low, so the total loss of an object may represent many years of premium payments. For instance, the premium to transport a nonfragile object valued at one hundred thousand dollars across the United States would be about thirty dollars, or 3/10 of 1 percent of its value: it would therefore take more than three thousand transits (or more than three thousand transit premiums) for the underwriter to recoup from a total loss of the object. No wonder insurance underwriters require high professional standards from museums.

Big art museums get a break because they have many objects at risk: they pay enough premiums to create a "pool" to help offset an occasional large loss. They can usually command broader coverage and an administratively flexible contract. Fine arts insurance specialists give automatic coverage of newly acquired items, transits, and small exhibitions, as well as coverage of employee dishonesty, breakage of fragile objects, and much more. They even allow the registrar to issue a "memorandum and certificate" of coverage that makes the lender to the museum a "named insured" under the museum's contract. All of these refinements are part of risk management; they serve either to broaden or to restrict the amount of risk the museum need take.

The most critical insurance choice the museum makes is its overall limit of liability. While some newer museums have an accurate estimate of the overall value of their collections, older, larger institutions seldom even know how many objects they hold, let alone their value. Now, with the assistance of computers, museums have the opportunity to come to grips with their actual exposure to risk.

There probably are only a few museums in the country that are insured to the actual value of their collections. There may be no reason to do so. The question prudent museum managers pose is: how much risk can the museum afford to share with the insurance company? While museums may not be able to insure the total collections for their actual value, a formula can be applied to gauge appropriate insurance levels.

A useful concept that helps determine the limit of liability is "probable maximum loss" or PML. If a fire swept through the museum wing that houses the most precious objects, what would be the overall value of the objects destroyed? The answer is the PML. There are various ways to alter the PML. If a museum moves its whole collection into one room, the PML rises; if it distributes values evenly between different parts of the building, the PML drops. Reducing the PML is one way of relieving risk. There are many reasons, practical and legal, to insure to the PML, but few museums do. Administrators who fail to insure to the PML assume a personal risk: in the event of a catastrophe, the courts may decide that an official who did not adhere to the "standard of reasonable care" is liable for the amount of a loss.

International Exhibitions

Another way to share the risk, at least on international exhibitions, is to let Uncle Sam bear part of it. In 1975, Congress passed the Arts and Artifacts Indemnity Act to assist museums that borrow from, or lend to, foreign institutions. At present, the cap on this government insurance program is $1.2 billion at risk at *any one time*. The ceiling on a single exhibition is $125 million. Soaring art prices—single paintings can now be worth as much as $50 million—have led many exhibition planners to wonder whether indemnification limits are realistic.

To apply for indemnity, museums submit detailed applications to the National Endowment for the Arts. The applications are in themselves important exercises in risk management and may take months to complete. The application is then reviewed by an advisory panel. The panel is usually far more restrictive than insurance companies. If the valuation of an art object is considered too high, the object will receive only partial indemnification. Some types of objects, such as works on wood panels, will not be indemnified at all. There is also a mandatory deductible of at least fifteen thousand dollars and up to fifty thousand. Indemnity during transit is limited to $20 million per conveyance.

Fine arts insurance fills the gap when a museum feels that indemnity coverage is inadequate. Insurance can provide coverage for amounts in excess of indemnity limits, for objects turned down by the indemnity program, or for the mandatory deductible amount. With values skyrocketing, museums mounting international blockbusters use both indemnity and commercial insurance policies. Despite its limitations, the indemnity program is a success. In fiscal year 1987, for example, 3,182 objects in twenty-seven exhibitions were indemnified to the tune of over $1.5 billion. Were there no indemnity program, insurance premiums paid out for these exhibitions would have totaled nearly $6 million.

Planning is Vital

How well a museum handles a loss depends on how well its risk managers planned for the crisis. Any loss, large or small, requires attention to myriad details and the expenditure of resources—time, staff, and money—on coping with the after-effects.

Museum risk managers should have the answers to the many questions that arise after disaster strikes. How fast can staff get to off-site copies of collections records? How much cash is available to deal with the loss? Who is empowered to authorize an emergency bank loan to carry out salvage and conservation? Who can be counted on to perform sensitive jobs like removing fragile objects from harm? How much community support is available to help rebuild the museum and its collections?

A museum is a dynamic place and its risk exposures are constantly changing. Risk management decisions made last year may not be adequate to protect the museum today. A responsible risk manager keeps pace with the evolving nature of the collections and of exhibition and storage practices. Furthermore, losing a collections piece means never to replace it. This is a tragedy not only for the museum but for the public. Risk management, therefore, is part of the museum's trust responsibility.

Risk and the Registrar

Because registrars work across departmental lines, they have a keen sense of the many stresses to which collections are subject; they are also familiar with what their colleagues need and expect from a collections management system. Registrars are concerned about both physical care and intellectual access to collections; they can weigh these demands against each other and come up with procedures to guarantee access with the least possible exposure. Registrars, because of their frequent contact with other institutions as well as with insurers, have a fund of knowledge about potential risk and risk prevention. They are in an ideal position to advise administrators on the ways to reduce exposure and on available risk-sharing options.

The registrar's insight and experience are critical to museum risk management, and can make the difference between a fragmented and a unified approach. Today's museum can no longer afford to address risk merely at the departmental level, but needs a cohesive strategy for the whole museum. Only this will provide a reasonable margin of safety. The registrar makes a crucial contribution to this goal.

Automation

Introduction to Automation

A s the 1980s draw to a close and registrars look back at what the decade has brought to their profession, they see many important changes. Among these are the adaptation of planning strategies from the business world and significant technical improvements in packing and shipping materials. The most far-reaching change, however, is still occurring: the development of new methods to manage information. These methods are made possible by the computer.

Not so long ago a computer was an event. Seldom seen, computers were huge machines hidden away in mysterious government agencies or vast corporations, or displayed in university buildings. Today, everyone is familiar with the blinking monitor, the clicking keys, the electronic whir of the disk drive. Ubiquitous, sometimes infuriating, computers have arrived. They have transformed our lives and our ways of working, and for the conceivable future, they are here to stay.

The computer offers solutions to many of the problems that registrars normally encounter. It brings order to the mass of information we handle. It organizes for us, replaces drawers of catalogue cards, and provides instant answers to questions people ask about collections objects.

The computer is a wonderful tool for collections information managers. The machine does certain tasks better than people can. Because it does not become bored, the computer carries out repetitive tasks with greater accuracy. It is fast. Because it serves as a central repository for data, it allows for speedy retrieval and quick updating. The computer saves space, paper, and time; it keeps data organized.

The computer does not replace the human brain. It does not think or plan, but it may help people make decisions. It matches like patterns of electrical impulses: those the user solicits with those already stored.

Developing an effective computerized collections information management system is done by people, not by machines. For the individual user, with a particular set of problems to solve, not just any computer will do. The task at hand determines the tool, the right machine and its programs. A wire whisk will whip cream, but a rotary beater is faster. A blender may be just right, depending on the amount of cream, but a food processor may be excessive. Microcomputers can perform some collections management tasks; but other tasks require a larger machine, especially in a large institution. In either case, the initial investment requires both time and money, but the long-term dividends are substantial. Increased productivity and improved morale are the first results of an effective system.

A computerized information system creates additional responsibilities for museum staff, particularly the registrar. Standards for data types and vocabulary must be maintained. The machine requires special care. Like a collection object, a computer needs a hospitable environment: temperature and humidity controls, lack of dust, protection against fire, flood, and theft, electrical outlets, and sometimes telephone lines. As a composite object, it requires several conservators, usually one for hardware, another for operating software, and sometimes a third for applications software.

The computer also expands systems documentation and security needs. Clear instructions and a set of operating procedures show the user how to make the computer perform each task. Security features exist to insure that only authorized persons gain access to the data. To prevent loss, backup copies of the data and the programs are securely stored at another site.

Appropriate training is essential. If users do not follow standard operating procedures, the desired results will not be forthcoming. Improper use of an automated system is a waste of resources, and an unskilled user can destroy the integrity of the data. Despite complexities and potential difficulties, filing, retrieving, and updating are so speeded by the machine that the computer becomes preferable to manual methods.

The use of computers in other aspects of contemporary life—banking, sales, order fulfillment, travel—has raised the expectations of both the museum community and the public about the sophistication and availability of collections information. Museums are more accountable for their holdings. National programs such as museum accreditation have raised the standards for museum records. Furthermore, information is a resource that increases the demand for itself. Meeting this demand requires the proper tool—carefully chosen computing systems equal to the challenge. Used properly, thoughtfully, and creatively, the computer can help fill the complex information needs of the museum and its public.

The Binary Ball Game

VIRGINIA MANN

Every registrar knows that manual record keeping is on the way out. After a long and venerable history extending back to antiquity, the practice of using a sharp instrument and a flat surface—a pointed stick and a clay tablet, a pencil and paper—is receding into oblivion. Manual systems, for all their ease and sophistication, are less and less capable of yielding answers to the questions registrars ask. The mountain of data is simply too big, the information needs too complex.

It was in the 1970s that museums entered the information age, and began to launch projects to computerize collections records. Some were successful and still exist. Many were dumped as failures, or were too costly, or were put on hold.[1] Nevertheless, every year more museums acquire computers, hoping to bring greater order to their collection of eight thousand chipmunk specimens or eighty thousand nearly identical Mayan beads. Registrars greet this development with both trepidation and relief.

Keeping electronic records is a whole new ball game. The registrar must re-examine every detail of the manual system. What data elements should be included in the automated system? How should they be formatted? Suddenly, consistent vocabulary is crucial. Authority lists, which provide the canonical form of an entry, must be developed. Should it be Maurice B. Prendergast or Maurice Brazil Prendergast? When should you use upper case and lower case, plural or singular, and how are special characters such as & or / to be used? What should be coded or not coded? Is Mesoamerica a continent or a culture?

A manual system is forgiving but limited. A computerized system is unforgiving and unlimited. Record keeping ideas that were never previously explored surface on a sea of possibilities. If the museum has a wide range of collections—ancient, oriental, ethnographic, decorative arts—are there terms that embrace each or does each collection require special treatment?

Take a straightforward painting:

1979.7.15
George Caleb Bingham (American, 1811–1879)
Boatman on the Missouri, 1846
oil on canvas
25⅛″ x 30⅜″ (63.8 x 77.3 cm)
Gift of Mr. and Mrs. John D. Rockefeller III

The accession number *as it stands* will not be sorted numerically by the computer. Assuming you cannot change the accession number you create another data field that contains the accession number in a form the computer orders as a human does: 1979.0007.0015. The number of decimal places depends on the number of estimated annual acquisitions. Should you start numbering objects newly received into the collection this way? How should the artist's name be entered: BINGHAM, George Caleb? If you use upper case for the last name, what will happen to Di Cione, Jacopo? From this, how will the user know whether the DI is Di or di? Or should it be entered CIONE, Jacopo Di, or not in upper case at all? Should you record the artist's nationality as an adjective, American, or should you use the country name, United States? Or United States of America? Or USA? The curator prefers Hopi "Indian" for the Americas and Maori "People" for Oceania: how can these language differences be preserved? The questions go on.

If data is entered into a computer inconsistently it will be lost during specific searches. Programs can be written to search for variations in spelling and format but complex and subtle variations require extensive, specific programming. Extra programs take disk storage space and lower the system's efficiency.

When a museum begins to computerize, nomenclature immediately plays a heightened role. Authority lists—approved terminology—become the heated topic of extensive committee meetings. No two people or two committees will derive the same authority list. Assume that a list includes the terms MARINE, LANDSCAPE, FIGURE, GENRE, STILL LIFE, PORTRAIT, and HISTORY as the primary set. The museum decides that the cataloguer must select one term only. Is Bingham's painting GENRE or FIGURE? Maybe LANDSCAPE? What if there are secondary, and even tertiary terms that might apply, such as RIVER or RIVER/MISSOURI, or BOAT? What kind of boat is it? If the museum elected to categorize by boats, then will an engraving of a boat on a silver tray qualify? Will a ship model in the collection be included, or does this terminology apply only to full-scale objects or only to images?

When developing authority lists museums tend to adopt their traditional manual systems. Eventually, the realization strikes that a computer can classify in countless ways. Traditional systems are often found to be restrictive—and they are frequently illogical and difficult to convert.

What about object type? A painting is a PAINTING and furniture is FURNITURE. What is a lamp? Is it best classified under function, as LIGHTING DEVICE, or FURNISHING? Or maybe even FURNITURE? If the lamp is glass, perhaps it should be categorized under GLASS, which is a traditional way to consider decorative art objects.

If a museum requires an object classification system, a nomenclature for that must also be developed. Should an object be classified according to function or for the reason it was collected? Should the painted trade sign be classified as ADVERTISING MEDIUM (its original purpose) or as FOLK ART (the reason the museum collected it)? Are we more interested in the jadeness or the jewelryness of a jade bracelet?

Decorative arts and ethnographic artifacts raise more questions. An English ceramic bowl is traditionally searched for under CERAMIC; likewise; an American wood object is classified under WOODWORK; and objects such as fire screens and fire tools are classified as METALWORK. An ethnographic object will be classified by functional type, as DOMESTIC OBJECT or under TOOLS AND IMPLEMENTS, for example. Complicating the rules are exceptions such as the term FURNITURE; which spans ancient, eastern, and ethnographic boundaries.

And how about the object that appears this way in the register:

71.16
Fetish, late 19th–early 20th century
Basonage, Belgian Congo, Africa
Wood
24″ x 5″ Museum purchase, M.H. DeYoung Art Trust Fund

Since the Belgian Congo is now Zaire, should this object be classified by place under the country name that was associated with it when it was made, or under the name of the country as it exists now? Or should the system include two or more data fields for country name? What happens to the country names in the coming centuries?

Is this fetish a piece of sculpture, or is it a ceremonial object? Why not allow for two (or three) object terms? Or is a primary classification with cross-references preferable? Is CEREMONIAL OBJECT the best term to use, or is RITUAL OBJECT or SOCIETAL ARTIFACT preferable? How does one classify amulets? Are they PERSONAL ARTIFACTS, COSTUME, or RITUAL OBJECTS? What is a mummy?

When museums were young, record keeping was simple. A typical ledger entry at the turn of the century may have used as few as six pieces (or fields) of information to describe an object. A subsequent entry may have had fewer or more (as well as different) data recorded. Today museums maintain hundreds of information fields about a single object, including technique of manufacture, hallmark, motif, medium, exhibition and photographic references, weight, valuation history, frame or accessory data, artist's birth and death places and dates, name of tribe, title in a foreign language, provenance, and countless other references. With the exception of title, each field requires an authority list or special instructions to guide data entry. On-line retrieval is a mirror image of the entry, or recording, process. You get out exactly what you put in.

In a history museum or historical site, collections are regarded as examples of material culture and are studied and searched under attributes that differ from those works of art or scientific specimens. A costume in an art museum may be collected and classified because of the designer. In a history museum the equivalent costume may be collected because it was worn by the First Lady to an inaugural ball. For future data exchange and comparative analysis how can the two different museums assure that common information about both costumes will be recorded?

The Linnaean system of classification for natural science specimens makes some of these problems less knotty. But museums may need to create other systems to deal with changing perceptions and concerns. Will rocks collected near nuclear power plants, for example, need some sort of environmental designation? For film collections, another set of systems must be invented. Multiple, edited copies must be differentiated; countless names of directors, actors, and camera crew members must appear; subjective and objective descriptions are pertinent. For a contemporary art museum new vocabulary is constantly added to accommodate new forms, new materials, and new concepts. The problems inherent in the classification of objects of popular culture boggle the mind. Will there be Coca-Cola, old Coke, new Coke, Classic Coke?

Registration in the modern museum is characterized by precise analysis of manual information systems developed over many decades. Registrars know that these systems possess the organizational memory. Changes to the systems are carefully considered and done for pragmatic reasons. Museums today are converting traditional record keeping systems to electronic medias to enhance efficiency and to maintain the record in the face of increased demand. Proficiency with the tools is the ticket for registrars to enter the electronic ball game.

Note

[1]Lenore Sarasan, "Why Computer Projects Fail," *Museum News* 59, no. 4 (January/February 1981): 40–49.

Thinking about Technology and Managing the Change

LOUISE JONES

In the early days of the automobile, Daimler-Benz discovered that the limited supply of trained chauffeurs would restrict potential sales. The company's response was to develop a car that could be driven by anyone, not just chauffeurs, mechanics, or engineers. In today's jargon, the car became user-friendly, and what was at first a technological novelty became a part of daily life.

Learning to use a new technology is intimidating. It is hard to remember that not only cars but even telephones and televisions were met by a certain degree of resistance. Some of us have grandparents who were reluctant or even afraid to use a phone; for our generation, it is the computer that sometimes gives rise to sweaty palms and an oppressive sense of inadequacy.

Though computers are all around us—at the office, the bank, the travel agency—there are numbers of people who know very little about these useful tools. Many of these people will soon learn about computers to conduct daily business. This is true of everyone who manages information. It includes museum registrars, whose stock in trade is managing information about collections. Though only a fraction of America's museums have adopted computerized collections management, the number is on the rise. Learning about technology, then, is one of the challenges that the museum registrar must face.

Computers come in many shapes and sizes, from the businessman's lap top personal computer to the huge mainframe. The machine is called the hardware; the programs that direct the hardware to process information in various ways are the software. Software has various functional capabilities: word processing and financial management programs are among the most widely used. But no matter the application, the essential task of the computer is to handle information, or rather, to allow the user to handle information, quickly and efficiently.

Over the last twenty years, computers have become familiar and valuable tools. Nevertheless, there remains a computer mystique. The media presentation of computers helped create an image of powerful, difficult, "thinking" machines with superhuman capabilities. Movies depict headstrong computers running amuck, or computers as instruments of malevolent forces. Good entertainment perhaps, but not conducive to making the uninitiated feel comfortable with the new technology.

In everyday life, the computer mystique translates into "technophobia," a condition often based on erroneous beliefs about what it takes to operate a computer. For example, many potential users of these new information-handling devices believe that they must be mathematically proficient, learn how to write programs, or even how to design and construct a computer before they can use it. Nothing could be farther from the truth.

Just as I can call Los Angeles without understanding how a phone works, so can I prepare a mailing list using a computer without a clear notion of microchip processing or how it enables me to do this task. Just as I can take a book out of the library without understanding the intricacies of the Library of Congress cataloguing system, so can I use the computer to find information on a carved trade sign in my museum without understanding semi-conductors, electrical circuits, or boolean algebra. I don't have to know the programming language that miraculously allows me to find out that the sign was loaned twice in the last decade. In short, I do not have to acquaint myself with the scientific knowledge that went into the development of computers, nor must I understand the design of the system that allows me the access to the information I seek. What I do need to understand is what the computer can do and what I must do to get it to work.

Broad acceptance of computers thus depends on whether potential users think they will be able to use the tool easily. It also depends on the selection of the hardware and the selection of the software: the key element is a program that enables the user to make the computer deliver on its promises.

There are two different kinds of designs for computers. A computer can perform a few vendor-defined functions or it can perform large numbers of user-defined functions. Computers that allow users to define functions by writing programs are known as general purpose computers. Computers with a few vendor-defined functions are known as special purpose computers. Word processors and automatic teller machine systems are examples of special purpose computer systems. Most people are quite comfortable using typing, printing, and editing functions provided by the stand-alone hardware and user-friendly software of a word processor. Similarly, many people use automatic teller machines for a variety of routine banking functions, and view these as machines for the deposit or withdrawal of money rather than as complex computer systems.

General purpose computers differ from special purpose computers by providing functions, or programming languages, for developing user-defined functions, or application programs. Thus, general purpose computers are universal information-handling tools with the ability to perform any function that the user can think clearly about, define, and construct as a program. The set of functions is potentially unlimited and of overwhelming complexity.

Fortunately, potentially complex general purpose computers can be converted into simple, manageable special purpose machines. This is routinely done when the user buys appropriate programs for information-handling functions. A well-equipped microcomputer in a mid-size museum registrar's office might use off-the-shelf software for budget preparation, for address label production, and for word processing. Each of these functions requires a separate software package. Managers who view computers as tools to get work done often choose this strategy.

It is a sound approach for museum registrars concerned with managing collections information.

It would seem that registrars, as a class, are the ideal users of the information age technology. Over the years, they have adopted or developed various manual systems to manage collections information. They know the principles of information and data management; they also know that the key to accurate, complete, and timely information is the structure of the information system.

What is meant here by structure? Imagine a personal information system, say a desk calendar. Appointments, reminders of special events, or daily expenditures appear by month, week, and day. This is a hierarchical arrangement: first the month, then the week, then the exact date. Another familiar personal information system, the checkbook, exhibits a sequential structure. Here the user retrieves data (expenses paid by check, deposits, funds available) in sequence—by check number or date.

While the information managed by computers may be collections information in a museum, employee information in a personnel department, supplies information in a storeroom, and customer and sales information in a marketing office, the basic functions and data structures of the systems are essentially the same. Every information system must allow for entering and determining the validity of data, as well as storing, accessing, and retrieving data.

Thus, when getting started with computers, managers and users must concentrate on the data they want to manage. What is the nature of the data? What functions is the computer to perform? The answers to these questions point the way to the proper selection of hardware and software: the needs and purposes of the user determine the tool.

Managing the Change

Another important thing to think about is the effect of new technology on the people using it and on the organization where they work. One of the sources of computer anxiety is the accurate perception that along with computers comes change. The conversion from manual information handling to automated information handling alters the nature of the work place and the tasks to be accomplished. Just as the telephone altered the fundamentals of how we communicate with one another so the computer is revolutionizing how we work.

People respond to change in different ways. Some people enjoy change and the growth it brings. Others are less inclined to change, but still adapt quickly. The most assertive among us make change occur. But for many change is difficult. Some individuals feel that they have little or no ability to manage the change or shape its outcome. This nonassertive response to change is characterized by the emotional stages of denial, anger, bargaining, depression, and finally, integration. Integration comes only when the individual accepts responsibility for making the change.[1] Moving through these stages can be painful, nonproductive, even destructive. Managers contemplating automation must be sensitive to the psychological dislocation that occurs when people are required to alter their work habits.

Researchers have found that in environments of significant change, people need answers to four basic questions: Where am I going? How am I to get there? Who will I be when I arrive? Can I feel good about myself in the process? Skillful managers of institutional change help employees find the answers to these questions. Employees see the opportunity and become part of the new world. Ultimately, each individual assumes responsibility for the decision to change and acts as required in the new environment.

How is a manager to create favorable conditions for introducing computers into the work place? The first thing is to define what results are expected of the person who will use the tool. Second, specify what must be done to produce the expected result. Third, select a tool that not only satisfies the functional requirements of the application but also attracts the user's interest and enthusiasm. People resist tools perceived as cumbersome. Although "user-friendliness" and "ease of use" are usually system design objectives, one person may find a particular machine and program more congenial than another.

Introducing computers into the work place is a one-time effort with a beginning and an end. Successful projects are those that meet the expectations of all concerned with project results, costs, and schedules. Successful projects produce information systems that work, and are completed on time and within budget. Most of all a successful project results in an enthusiastic user prepared to handle the system.

Such a project requires a well-articulated yet flexible work plan. This will help insure coming in on time and within budget. The work plan should include a schedule based on forty- to eighty-hour tasks; each task should have a tangible result with a specified quality standard. Managers should measure progress on the basis of completed work; the tangible result should meet the quality standard. Well-conceived project plans and schedules are powerful management tools.

Building user enthusiasm for the system requires an understanding of the learning curve characteristic of the adoption of any new technology. The first stage is the application of the technology to improve efficiency—people use the tool to do previously defined tasks faster. In the second stage people use the new technology to address old problems in new ways. The third, and final stage, consists of new applications—people use the tools to solve completely new problems.

It is important to let people know about this gradual but real progress. New users should be able to anticipate a future in which they have mastered the computer and transformed it into a willing and efficient servant. For the museum registrar, the technology will be enriching. Indeed, registrars can expect to find new and completely unanticipated ways to use computer-based information-handling tools.

The individual registrar who is thinking about computers can take steps to prepare for the selection and use of appropriate tools. Tutorials are available on videotape. Friendly computers, such as word processors, are available in non-threatening environments for experimentation. Finally, registrars can join together with their colleagues to address common information-handling problems.

In summary, when thinking about computers remember that they are meant to improve the performance of the systems registrars use to manage collections information. The information-handling tools selected should simplify the tasks and be easy to use. Finally, the project of integrating the new tool into the museum must assure that everyone affected by the change is committed to making it happen successfully.

Note

[1] Elisabeth Kubler-Ross, *On Death and Dying* (Macmillan: New York, 1970).

Computer Realities in Museums

JAMES CLIFFORD

W hat is the "state of the art" in museum computer usage? A recent survey[1] estimated that only 32 percent of American museums use computers at all. Primarily, museums use computers for administrative functions: only 16 percent of museums use computers for collections information management and most of this usage is for the simplest collections management tasks. Not surprisingly, the majority of museums surveyed indicated that they *plan* to use computers in some fashion in the future.

Museums use computer technology to disseminate information both externally and internally. Information flows to the public to increase both their access to, and their appreciation of, the material in the museum. Information flows to the museum staff to help them do their jobs more effectively.

Internal Functions

Internal uses of computer technology fall into three functional areas: office automation, collections management, and environmental control. Office automation tasks in a museum are much the same as in any office. Computerized systems such as electronic mail, calendars, word processing, and interactive teleconferencing are affordable realities. They are easily installed and easy to learn. Many museums are also beginning to automate business functions such as personnel, payroll, and accounting. Office automation, including the automation of financial systems, accounts for most of the computer usage in museums today. Finally, museums are also looking to computers to help manage mailing lists, membership records, and development efforts. These areas have nothing to do with the unique role of a museum.

In its unique role as a caretaker, a museum must record basic inventory information about each object in its holdings. There has been much museum interest and activity surrounding the automation of this important registration function. The Museum Computer Network existed for over a decade to advise museums considering or in the process of automating registration records. Software systems exist to support registration and many museums have initiated automated registration projects of varying degrees of complexity: not all have survived.[2]

The major tasks of the basic collections management function do not differ in principle from those of any inventory system. However, the tasks are influenced by the one exceptional feature that distinguishes a museum inventory from any other: objects and records seldom leave. Even when an object is deaccessioned, its record remains in the system. Thus the size of the database is constantly growing.

A look at the general file structure of a typical, basic collections management system in an art museum makes this clear:

- ACCESSION FILE: legal acquisition information about acquired objects
- OBJECT CATALOGUE FILE: descriptive data about objects in the museum's collections
- SOURCE FILE: information about each donor, vendor, or lender of museum objects, often including financial records
- LOANS/EXHIBITS FILE: records regarding specific objects on loan or on exhibit
- PHOTOGRAPH FILE: a record of photographs of each object, with basic data about the photograph
- INVENTORY FILE: location file on each object
- CONSERVATION FILE: conservation data on each object
- RESEARCH FILE: research data—history, provenance, exhibition history
- DISPOSITION FILE: data about the deaccessioning of objects

This information allows the museum to care for objects under its protection. Museum staff find information about the object's provenance, current location, physical condition, and legal and economic status in these files.

There are many automated systems in use to support these functions. Some are tailor-made for museums, other are general purpose inventory management systems, and general purpose database management systems. The development of the micro-computer, associated mass storage devices, and general-purpose software packages—all at reasonable prices—should bring au-tomated collections management within the reach of all but the most impecunious or most short-sighted of museums.

Automation of environmental control in the museum is less common. However, a few newly designed museums do make use of some of this technology. In the general commercial real estate market the buzzword of the eighties is "smart buildings." Although not yet a well-defined term, a smart building is one that has been wired with digital PBX (private branch exchange) or fiber optics cable and equipped with systems that supply a variety of enhanced communication and control services.

Among the services supplied or envisioned are: teleconfer-encing, telecommunications, and local area networks; energy systems such as automatic lighting, temperature, and humidity control; fire, smoke, and other hazard detection; voice com-munication at the building's entry points, elevators, stairwells, and other passage points; access to outside sources such as weather services and other information centers; and vastly increased communication capabilities to support video, voice, holo-graphic, and other multimedia devices.

Few smart buildings exist today, and the jury is still out on their economic feasibility. Nonetheless, the technology is here and some is becoming cost effective. As this technology enters the museum environment, registrars should take an active part in the early stages of new museum building projects.[3] They can contribute to planning the infrastructure to support the infor-mation needs of the museum of tomorrow.

Although there are hundreds of things to know about museum objects, the reality is that museums record very little information. An informal look at various museum computerization projects indicates that very few museums are recording more than a dozen or so of the literally hundreds of pieces of information of potential interest to the public. In the art world a bare information system records the object title, artist, execution date, medium, and dimensions. Slightly more sophisticated systems add inscription information, ownership history, and perhaps exhibition history and bibliographical references. The most elaborate systems include extensive biographical information on artists, and have adopted some sort of subject classification scheme. The database for the Yale Center for British Art, designed in the early 1970s, included all this information. At the time many considered it to be the most ambitious museum undertaking of this sort. But today many museums, including the one at Yale, have cut back on the information content of their databases because of the cost of collection, verification, and maintenance.

There is, of course, a wealth of recordable information about objects in a museum's care. Much of it is of interest to the general public, some of it is of interest only to researchers and scholars, but *all* of it is potentially of interest to someone. Not only is the amount of information extensive, it is all connected in a complicated web of interrelationships and crossreferences. This complex network of information might include:

- extensive art historical information, including every exhibition, every published reference, every related work of art in any medium

- information about the history of all the various artistic media, including references to published works on the medium, its earliest known use, videotapes of artists or craftsmen using the medium, conservation information pertaining to the medium

- extensive biographical data, not simply on artists but on everyone connected to the works of art, including publishers, engravers, subjects, art historians, and collectors

- controlled and extensive subject classifications including cross-references to information about the subjects, the history of the subjects, and the study of the subjects

The information potential is enormous. Museums have only begun to examine this potential, but the increasing demands of a growing public impels activity in this area. Many people do not regard simple facts as the best kind of information. People seek relationships, connections between simple facts, between one fact and another. The management of these interconnections is known as information linkage.

Information Linkage

An American history student, for example, using the museum's database, might be understandably frustrated when the museum's computer provides only facts previously known about an object: the manufacturer's name, its date and size, original function, material, and condition. What the student seeks is related information. What other objects were collected at the same time in the same geographic location? What other objects use a similar gearing mechanism? Did the manufacturer produce other object types? What was the distribution route? Who used the object? Who specifically and who as a "class" within the society at large? In short, when asking questions about a specific object the student is looking to the database to function as a real research tool, not simply as an inventory.

Related information is extensive. It might include historical facts about the period of the object's creation or discovery, or a list of exhibitions related to the object, or a discussion of the object's source, or bibliographical references. In the example above, a bibliographical reference could even lead the student to a book that contains the information he needs.

The problems with information linkage of this sort are many. Because there is so much related information, the data resist constraint. What data to include and what to ignore are delicate issues. Furthermore, it is incredibly time-consuming to discover, validate, and organize this information, to correct it, and to keep it current.

Storing all the possible connections between different categories of collections information is a monumental task. Exhibition histories, biographies, bibliographies; provenance; social and political history; scientific and technological developments; descriptions of artistic media: all these, and more, would have to be included. Information of a different kind, such as access paths to records in other museums, libraries, or archives, would have to be added as well. Isn't such an endeavor utterly cost-prohibitive?

Certainly it has been. The cost of storage media; of the research staff to discover, validate, and organize this information; of data entry clerks and proofreaders, of corrections and updates; the cost of searching, sorting, and printing! Can, will, or even should a museum or society pay these costs?

Leaving aside this question, there are at least three encouraging notes to sound. First of all, the costs of computing are coming down, and the capacity of storage is rising. This trend began when the first computers were built forty years ago, and it has continued unabated. Furthermore, experience teaches ingenious, inventive ways to reduce the liability in time, effort, and money. After building an initial museum database of information essential to basic operations, adding additional information and functions is proportionally less costly. Thus the information base should be seen as an organic repository that will grow and evolve over the years. Finally, as more cultural institutions automate information, it will become easier to beg, borrow, or otherwise acquire some of that knowledge through any of the myriad communication networks that are appearing. The international business community invests heavily in the building of international communication networks, and the technology and the standards needed to support them are finally emerging.

Today's museums, like most computer users, generally employ some form of screen for data entry and on-line querying, and a printer for hard copy output. This means that access by the public to the information ranges from minimal to nonexistent. Where public access exists, it is generally restricted to some printed record of the object, in printout or index card format. Access, as in some libraries, to on-line querying is very rare. Museums with first-generation collections management systems are only beginning to develop policies and procedures for allowing some form of public on-line access to information.

Screens and printouts, however, are anything but the whole story about input and output. Over the past decade many other forms of input and output devices and techniques have moved from the research laboratories and the universities into actual products—video disks are one example. Bar coding, almost universal in supermarkets, has implications for museum numbering and locating systems. Technologies emerging now will eventually enter the market. Museum professionals will have to make more educated choices, informed both by economic and educational considerations, as to which forms of human-machine communication are most appropriate.

Among the many possibilities are natural language communication, either typed or spoken. Built upon years of research exploring how to understand speech and language, many systems can now provide some form of natural language communication between users and the computer. The most effective allow virtually unrestricted English communication with database querying systems—exactly the environment appropriate for a dialogue between the public and the museum's information base. These systems will continue to improve.

The state of spoken natural language communication systems is less advanced, but mature systems are inevitable. Video disks already provide high-resolution color output, ideal for communicating images of art works both from within the museum's own collection and from outside sources. Combined with a photographic archive, this technology could be an unparalleled research tool. Elaborate and imaginative use of graphics and of color can combine with direct manipulation devices like the mouse, the light pen, and touch panels to produce astonishing effects. Techniques of zooming through video representations of the museum's collection, three-dimensional holographic images, and the ability to enlarge, reduce, or rotate an object electronically are possibilities. As museums acquire technological sophistication, imagination will, no doubt, find itself bounded only by finances.

Until now museum computerization efforts have focused on automating various internal functions performed by museum staff. With many first-generation museum information systems underway, museum professionals aspire to the challenges of automating communication between the public and their information bases.

The goal is to improve the museum programs by offering more and higher quality information to the public. The museum public spans the distance between visiting schoolchildren and scholars, between family outings and family pilgrimages, between those spending hours contemplating aesthetics and those wooed by the "Oh, WOW!" quality that museums embody. There are at least several aspects to consider when discussing improvement to public delivery of information: content, linkage, presentation, and security. Closely related concerns include determining the appropriate storage media, and insuring the integrity of the information.

Today's museum systems typically inhabit either in-house mini- or microcomputers, or they run in a time-shared environment on somebody else's mainframe. The storage media are surely magnetic—either hard or floppy disks for on-line work with magnetic tape storage for archival information and backups. The software systems are basically first generation database management systems: large, multi-user mainframe systems or one of the smaller database packages for the in-house microsystem. Data security, beyond whatever physical security system is in place (guards, keys, and the like) is usually not more complicated than a log-on password.

Progress continues unabated. The latest product in the storage array is the optical disk. Using laser technology to read and write permits a much greater density and speed than magnetic disks, yet costs compare favorably. Currently limited to a write-once technology, methods to mark errors and link corrections and additions have improved. For archival records—a substantial body in any museum—this is ideal technology. For more volatile environments, optical disks with rewrite capabilities will soon appear in the market place. The storage capacity of these laser disks outstrips that of the largest magnetic disks of today—clearly a boon to museums contemplating storing volumes of linked information. Finally, video disk technology combines mediums and presents pictures (moving or still), sound, and graphics.

Database management systems (DBMS) have matured in the last decade. Among the issues that received attention—beyond speed and cost considerations—are two that are relevant here. Tomorrow's DBMS will include subsystems specifically to provide data integrity and data security.

The integrity subsystem insures greater accuracy of the data by allowing automatic control of the interconnections among and between data. Integrity rules, defined by the database administrator, are automatically invoked and enforced by the system whenever there is relevant database activity. Integrity rules can be simple, such as: "The dimensions of an object must be numeric" or "Every person must have a gender, either M or F." But these rules can become more complex, expressing more interfield or interrecord relationships: "No object can have a person as an artist until there is a corresponding artist record in the biography file" or "If the title of the object is *Self Portrait*, then there should be a common person sorted as artist and proper subject." The automatic enforcement of such rules can greatly improve the accuracy and completeness of the information base.

The security subsystem insures that only people authorized to do so can access any piece of information. The database administrator defines who is authorized to perform what activity on what information. This is done for each piece of information, or for combinations of pieces, and for each type of activity—read, write, or modify. The "who" might be an individual user name, a class of people, such as "curatorial staff" or "database administrator" or even "everyone." Access might be further limited by constraints such as day of week and time of day: "Only Monday through Friday, between nine and five," by location: "Only from terminal thirty-seven in room 312." More elaborate user identification procedures will be available to further guarantee data security.

As museums begin to store greater and greater volumes of information, some more sensitive then others, and provide access to information owned by other institutions geographically dispersed, they will have to make more knowledgeable decisions about storage media and data security. Happily, these choices are plentiful.

Conclusions

What will the future museum be like? It would be presumptuous to make any but the most general conjectures. Nevertheless, one thing can be said with certainty: in the future technology will provide for much greater control and dissemination of the information that museums shelter. Developments will occur along three parallel paths. Technological refinements will support expanded modes of communication and cheaper, higher capacity storage. Museums will continue efforts towards standardization and cooperation, and increase commitment to imaginative, first-rate information systems. And society as a whole must make the economic commitment to support such an undertaking.

Society and the collective community of museums face this challenge. On balance it is hard to deny that the rewards are worth the risks. Each small step taken to improve the quality, the content, and the presentation of museum collections information will in the end justify itself.

Notes

[1] The Art Museum Association of America (AMAA), *Technology in Museum Environments: A National Survey of Current and Anticipated Computer Use in Art Museums* (San Francisco: AMAA, 1982).

[2]Lenore Sarasan, "Why Museum Computer Projects Fail," *Museum News* 59, no. 4 (January/February 1981): 40–49.

[3]David Vance, "Planning Ahead: The Registrar's Role in a Building Program," in *Museum Registration Methods*, eds. Dorothy H. Dudley et al. (Washington, D.C.: American Association of Museums, 1979), 395–408.

Computer Fantasies for Museums

JAMES CLIFFORD

Conjuring up fantasies about the museum of the future is a pastime open to all. What will technology bring? Let's wander in a world of possibilities.

Unseen by the security guard, you move stealthily towards the Sargent. Finally your dream of owning *The Portrait of Madame X* is coming to fruition. At last it will be yours! All of your plans have worked out perfectly. Reaching out with one hand to stabilize the picture, your other hand, holding the knife, nears the canvas to begin the cut that will free the treasure.

> "AAAHR-AAAHR-AAAHR-AAAHR
> SECURITY TO ROOM 6A.
> SECURITY TO ROOM 6A."

Unknown to you, everything in the museum—the floors, walls and ceilings, the stairwells, entrances and exits, the paintings, the sculpture and the object cases—is completely wired, forming one vast complex connected to the central computer, the "brain" of this nervous system, sensitive to your every movement. Within seconds security guards surround you. They lead you off to a detention room while the city police, already notified electronically, speed toward the museum. Your fantasy lies shattered, but the sophisticated computer technology in this "smart building" prevented an irreplaceable work of art from being lost to the public.

★   ★   ★   ★

It is 6:00 A.M. You wake up, at home in bed, and suddenly realize that although you have scheduled an 8:00 A.M. lecture

to a class of visiting students in the auditorium, you have forgotten to reserve the space. Reaching for the phone, you quickly
dial into the museum's telecommunications facility. With the
touch-tone pad of your phone, it is a simple matter to key in
the reservation: seminar name, date, time, and room. You heave
a sigh of relief as the office automation system accepts the reservation—there is no conflicting meeting! Now you can relax
for another thirty minutes, as the building maintenance system
begins to "wake up the building." It adjusts the lights, regulates
the temperature and prepares the building for another day.

★　★　★　★

It is 9:00 A.M. on Tuesday morning. Since the exhibition
you curated has just opened on Monday, you are understandably
anxious to know the first day's attendance figures. Picking up
your telephone, you touch "C" for computer.

"Hello, this is Veronica," you say. "How did the show do
yesterday?"

"Well, we had 653 people come into the museum, and out
of these, 512 people, or 78.4 percent came to see your exhibition."

"Well, that seems pretty good to me. But tell me, how did
the Etruscan exhibition do last year on its first day?"

"The Etruscan exhibition? Well, you did better in absolute
numbers and also in percentages. That one was seen by only
350 people out of the daily total of 585, which was 59.8 percent."

"Well, that's a relief. But could you please arrange to have
the daily figures on my desk each morning before I get in?"

"Will do."

★　★　★　★

As you walk into the Fine Arts Museum, the attendant hands
you a small, lightweight headset complete with mouthpiece.
"Just put it on and start talking," he says. "The computer will
serve as your guide through the museum." Putting it on, feeling
slightly uncomfortable, you mumble, "The computer?"

"Yes, I will be your guide," a voice responds through the
earphones. "Welcome to the Fine Arts Museum. Was there

something special that brought you here today?"

"Well, I've heard that you have some sort of special exhibition mounted, and I have some free time today."

"Oh, you must mean the Vatican exhibition. Would you like me to tell you something about it before we go up?"

"Sure. The Vatican, you say?"

"Yes. The exhibition is composed of nearly 250 pieces on loan from the Vatican in Rome, and will be seen in only three American cities before returning home. Many of the pieces are priceless masterpieces, reflecting the long and unique relationship between the Papacy and art. Because the exhibition traces the collecting traditions of the Vatican over many centuries, it provides a unique opportunity to view the changing taste, both in artistic and religious customs, of. . . ."

"Oh, do you mean there will be a lot of religious art?" you interrupt.

"Well, yes, but not entirely. You see. . . ."

"I'm not really in the mood for that! What else have you got going on today?"

★   ★   ★   ★

You need help. Last month one of the trustees went on vacation to Amsterdam and came back impressed by the cleaning and restoration of Rembrandt's *Night Watch*. He brought it up at the last trustee's meeting, and now the pressure is on to spruce up the one Rembrandt in your collection. You will have to bring in an expert, but you do know *something* about conservation, and you would like to be able to discuss the issues intelligently at next week's hastily called trustee's meeting, and also when you begin to contact conservators. Fortunately, your computer provides you with on-line access to the complete texts of a whole library of books, articles, and monographs.

Indicating the key words "Painting Conservation" to the SEARCH BY KEY WORD option on the menu, you find that there are approximately fifty references from which to choose. Two of them stand out as well-known classics in the field: George Stour's *The Care of Pictures* and Helmut Ruhemann's

The Cleaning of Paintings. You choose the latter and within a few moments its table of contents appears on the screen. You select the chapter on cleaning, and begin browsing through the vaguely familiar territory: surface cleansing; removal of varnish; removal of retouchings; alcohol, acetone, and turpentine. Well, this looks like just the thing and so you settle more snugly into your chair for a long afternoon of technical reading.

★ ★ ★ ★

You are a doctoral student doing research on the development of John Constable's landscape painting. The influences of Claude, Gainsborough, and Wilson are well documented, but you believe it was really Ruisdael, generally thought to be only a modest influence, who made the most profound contribution to the naturalism in Constable's mature work. To develop evidence to support your theory you must view first-hand as many works by both artists as possible.

London, with its wealth of galleries, is the prime location for viewing the Constables, and it will serve as the home base for your planned trip to Europe. What you need to find out is the location of other sizable collections of Ruisdaels. The computer information base at the university museum is of immense help. Entering "Ruisdael" as the search key word, you find out (no news to you!) that your own gallery has one oil painting, four watercolors, and about twenty or so prints after Ruisdael originals. Choosing first the OTHER COLLECTIONS option presented to you, and then the BY COUNTRY option, you discover that within Europe, Great Britain itself is rich in Ruisdaels, primarily in Birmingham, Cambridge, Edinburgh, and London. By far the largest concentration, however, is in the Netherlands. Scattered in several museums in Amsterdam are roughly thirty, with eight more in Rotterdam.

Clearly, it makes sense to combine your trip to Great Britain with a long excursion to the Netherlands. As it turns out, Paris and Brussels also have a number of Ruisdaels, and so your itinerary is taking shape. Before leaving the information center, you stop to pick up the print-out you have requested—a list of all the known Ruisdaels in Great Britain, the Netherlands, Paris, and Brussels.

★ ★ ★ ★

Arriving at the museum after a long day at work, you are to be forgiven if, upon seeing the crowd waiting on line at the entrance, you are unable to prevent a mild expletive from crossing your lips. Composing yourself, you ask the guard, "How long will I have to wait?" Looking at his computer screen, he tells you that there are currently 825 people in the exhibition area, which is divided into four rooms now occupied by 220, 242, 308, and 55 people, respectively. "Ten more people can now come in," he announces. As they enter, he returns to you and says that the average waiting time today has been forty-five minutes, but that in the last hour this has increased to fifty-seven minutes. The average time to walk through the exhibition has been consistent all day—just under one hour. You look at your watch and do some quick arithmetic; you will have just about enough time to see the show and make your dinner date. "Do me a favor and keep me posted if there is any change in these statistics," you say. You re-take your place in line, reassured by the sense that you are not simply waiting completely in the dark.

★ ★ ★ ★

"I am interested in Max Ernst," you say to the friendly looking man at the information desk. "Do you have any of his paintings on exhibit?" "I believe we do," he answers, "But why don't you just ask our computerized information center?" He points to the group of display terminals to his right. "It can give you the most up-to-date information." At the terminal, you type in "Max Ernst." Immediately the reply appears on the screen.

The museum owns twelve paintings and three sculptures by Max Ernst; four painting and two pieces of sculpture are on public display. You can get more information on any of the holdings by moving the cursor to the title and clicking the mouse. If you would like to learn more about the artist himself,

choose ARTIST. For information on Ernst works in other locations, you can choose ELSEWHERE; and finally, for information related to Ernst, choose RELATED INFORMATION.

Clicking the mouse with the cursor on *Two Children Being
Pursued by a Nightingale* produces a short paragraph of information about the painting, including medium ("oil on wood
with wood construction"), execution date ("1924"), and dimensions ("27½ x 22½ x 4½ inches"). It is located on the second
floor in gallery 207, but you can view it on the video display
if you like. Choosing this option, a color image of the object
instantly appears on the monitor.

After viewing a number of objects in the collection in this
manner, you are delighted to discover that, even for such an
object as *Swamp Angel*, which is located across the globe in
Rome, you are able to see a color reproduction (in this case,
the color has been computer-generated from a black-and-white
photograph of the object). You would eventually like to travel
to Rome to see the actual object, but this is the next best thing.
In fact, the system informs you, fully 80 percent of the known
Ernst *oeuvre* is viewable on the monitor before you!

Next you choose BIOGRAPHY INFORMATION. This
presents you with a text browsing system, which displays a
piece of text and highlights all the terms that have separate entries
in the system. You can keep moving forward through any piece
of text, which in your case begins with a biography of Ernst,
but you can also at any time migrate to related entries (high-
lighted in **bold**) which elaborate on any of the first set of high-
lighted terms. Browsing through the database, you wander
through entries on *Bruhl*, Ernst's birthplace on the *Rhine*, and
Bonn, where he studied and became interested in **abnormal
psychology**. Some of the artists whose works influenced him
and the school of *Dadaism* were *de Chirico, Jean Arp*, and *George
Grosz*. Among the many **media** in which Ernst worked were
collage, pastel, bronze, and *pencil frottage*; you browse through
entries on their history and techniques.

Finally, choosing the RELATED INFORMATION option,

you discover that the system has information on about eighty-five other works of art that are related to works by Ernst, and references to over three hundred books, articles, and monographs that shed light on the artist and his work. Choosing the BOOKS option, the Library of Congress catalogue information on thirteen books appears on the screen, as well as information on which local libraries have copies. You are even given the option of automatically keying into the circulation system of one of the local libraries, and could have the book immediately reserved for you to pick up.

★   ★   ★   ★

You have been dreading this moment. Today is the day that you must go into the storeroom to get those eight jars of fish specimens that are to be shipped off to some country you have never even heard of for study.

Logging onto the system, you discover that the ROBOT CONTROL option has been added to your menu. You've never needed it before and hadn't even noticed it, but now it turns out to be the option you choose. Proceeding in similar fashion through the sequence of menus presented to you, you indicate that you want SPECIMEN RETRIEVAL. Keying in the accession numbers, the system displays the registrar's file for each accession, allowing you to verify that these are, indeed, the desired fish. Finally, after indicating that the destination is the examination and packing room, you courageously select the GO option. Automatically, using the location, size, and physical container descriptors, the robotics system begins to carry out its assigned task.

Minutes later, you "self-propel" your mere human form to the examination room, somewhat incredulous but determined not to be skeptical. There the robot is just delivering the first of the successfully retrieved jars to a member of the packing crew! An hour later the entire job is finished.

★   ★   ★   ★

Probably not all of our brushes with the technological marvels of the near-future will be as smooth as these. Nevertheless, new and powerful allies are waiting to help museum staff do their jobs with greater ease, to raise standards of collections management, and to better serve the public. The fantasies captured here are only a few versions of the actualities that time will bring. Look around your own museum—and dream of the possible.

Glossary

ACCESSION. (1) An object, or group of objects, acquired by a museum as part of its permanent collection. (2) The act of recording/processing an addition to the permanent collection. *Accession Number.* A control number, unique to an object, whose purpose is identification, not description. It is part of the numbering system for the museum's permanent collection and records the transaction whereby an object enters the collection. The accession number is based on the object's order of acceptance into the permanent collection (not on the class of the object). It consists of the year of accession and a serial number.

ACCREDITATION. The American Association of Museums (AAM) accredits museums that meet certain professional standards. The AAM's accreditation program has as its goal to establish and maintain these professional standards and to evaluate museum organizations in the light of those standards.

AIR RIDE. The suspension system of a truck or trailer that uses air bags rather than metal springs. This cushion of air absorbs road shocks and provides a smoother ride.

AIRWAYBILL. The basic shipping document in air freight; it is both the contract of carriage between the shipper and carrier and the receipt for the shipment.

APPLICATIONS SOFTWARE. Computer program designed to perform specific tasks, such as word processing or database management.

AUTHORITY LIST. Common set of records identifying a standard for established forms of headings, index terms, or other items that are used for information retrieval. May also contain established cross-references.

BUG CHAMBER. An environmentally controlled area designed for the purpose of preparing mammal and other vertebrate skeletons by removing the flesh from the bones. It is called a bug chamber because beetles are introduced into the area to consume the carrion.

BYTE. In computer terminology, a unit of data storage representing one character of information.

CATALOGUE. (1) a museum's file comprised of cards, one or more for each object in its permanent collection. (2) A publication listing and describing objects in an exhibition or collection. (3) The act of classifying objects methodically, usually with descriptive detail.

CHARACTER SET. A finite set of designated characters, or bytes, used for codifying, usually by computer.

COCKLING. A broad wrinkle or system of wrinkles without creasing, usually referring to the conformation of paper or parchment.

COLLECTION. Refers to the objects, specimens, documents, and data under a museum's care.

CONDITION REPORT. Statement describing the exact physical state of an object, usually derived from a visual examination.

CONSERVATION REPORT. Statement describing the physical condition of an object, including proposed or executed treatment, based on an examination using appropriate scientific techniques.

DATA STANDARD. Criteria established to ensure data integrity.

DEACCESSION. (1) An object that has been removed permanently from a museum collection, usually through sale or exchange. (2) The process of removing an object permanently from the collection.

DIGITAL DISK. A thin flat circular plate on which data is stored in digital format; decoded by laser technology.

DOCUMENTATION. (1) The physical record of information relating to a museum object. (2) The process of creating records pertaining to each object in a museum collection.

DONATION. A gift or contribution. In a museum, usually money or negotiable securities, material to be accessioned into the permanent collection or to be used for educational purposes, or gifts of in-kind services or material.

DONOR RESTRICTION. Limit or restraint placed on a gift by the donor. In a museum, donor restrictions are undesirable as they usually hamper use of the gift by museum managers.

EXCLUSIVE USE. When a consignor or shipper purchases use of the entire truck or freight container; no other freight may be added.

EX-COLLECTION. Collection to which a museum object formerly belonged.

FIBER OPTIC. The technology of transmitting data over communication lines made from flexible strands of glass or plastic through which laser beams or light is passed.

FIBER OPTIC CABLE. Fiber optic strands bundled to form a cable that can carry many more times the amount of data than traditional copper wire.

FOXING. A discoloration of paper caused by the action of mold on iron salts, which are present in most paper; usually the result of high relative humidity.

FUNCTIONAL TYPE. Classification of museum objects based on the function, or use, or the object.

HARD DISK. An electronic data storage device that uses a disk made of a rigid base (plastic, ceramic, aluminum) and coated with a magnetic material.

INTERNATIONAL COUNCIL OF MUSEUMS (ICOM). A professional organization founded in 1946 and dedicated to the improvement and advancement of the world's museums. Headquartered in Paris, ICOM's representative in the United States is housed by the American Association of Museums.

INTERNATIONAL STANDARDS ORGANIZATION (ISO). Headquartered in Geneva, ISO promotes the development of standardization throughout the world. Its goal is to facilitate the international exchange of goods and services, and to develop cooperation in intellectual, scientific, technological, and economic activity.

INVENTORY. (1) An itemized list of objects for which a museum has assumed responsibility through either accession or loan. (2) The process of physically locating objects for which the museum is responsible and reconciling the location data with previous records.

I/O CONFIGURATION. Input/output standards designating the process of entering data into the computer or of transferring data from computer to a printer, terminal, or storage medium.

LASER DISK. An information storage medium using a controlled laser beam to expose areas on a photosensitive surface. When the laser beam is interrupted, a desired information pattern results.

LIGHT PEN. In computer graphics, a light-sensitive device that is pointed at the display surface and used to draw, or to engage a computer activity.

LOCAL AREA NETWORK (LAN). A system of connecting computers, word processors, and other electronic office machines to create an interoffice or intersite network.

MAGNETIC DISK. A flat circular plate layer, used for storing electronic data coated with magnetic material, on which data and programs can be stored.

MAIN FRAME. A large computer, often the hub of a system serving many users; an excellent resource base when many users need similar information.

MATRIX. The rock or main substance in which a crystal, mineral, or fossil is embedded and in which the impression remains.

MEGABYTE. One million bytes or eight million bits.

MOUSE. Small, hand-held device that can be moved over the surface of a magnetically sensitive surface, causing the computer's cursor to move to a corresponding point on the screen.

MUSEUM. An organized and permanent nonprofit institution, essentially educational or aesthetic in purpose, with professional staff, which owns and utilizes tangible objects, cares for them and exhibits them to the public in some regular manner.

NATIONAL ENDOWMENT FOR THE ARTS (NEA). An independent agency of the federal government with goals to foster artistic excellence by helping to develop national creative talent, preserve the cultural heritage, make the arts available to a wider, more informed audience, and to promote the overall financial stability of American arts organizations.

NATIONAL ENDOWMENT FOR THE HUMANITIES (NEH). An independent agency of the federal government that stimulates the growth and development of the humanities in the United States by awarding grants to individuals and organizations.

NOMENCLATURE. A system for naming objects. In history museums, often refers to Robert G. Chenall's *Nomenclature for Man-Made Objects* (Nashville: American Association for State and Local History, 1978), which classifies objects by functional type.

OBJECT. Used throughout *Registrars on Record* to include the variety of things museums include in their collections — works of art, natural specimens, film, photographs, decorative arts, implements, tools, etc.

OPERATING SOFTWARE. Computer program that controls basic and initial, and generic computer operations; may provide scheduling, debugging, input/output control, accounting, compilation, storage assignment, data management, and related services.

OPTICAL DISK. A grooveless disk on which digital data (text, music, or pictures) is stored as tiny pits in the surface and is decoded by a laser beam scanning the surface.

PBX (PRIVATE BRANCH EXCHANGE). A private telephone switching system usually located on the user's premises. This system provides intrapremises exchange telephone service as well as access to the public exchange network and/or private facilities.

POLYURETHANE. A polymer with a light foamy texture resulting from the entrapment of carbon dioxide in pores during production. Frequently used in packing materials.

PRO FORMA INVOICE. An estimate of costs and expenses that is delivered prior to determining actual costs and expenses.

PROGRAMMING LANGUAGE. A set of characters or symbols combined to produce commands and rules, with meanings assigned to their use for writing computer programs. Examples are COBOL, BASIC, and FORTRAN.

RECOVERY. The amount of money available to a museum in lieu of a lost or damaged object.

RELATIONAL DATABASE. A database in which relationships between data are explicitly specified as equally accessible attributes.

SUBLOCATION. In a museum, usually refers to the specific drawer or shelf where an object is permanently stored. For example: room S34, cabinet 18 (location), D4 (sublocation).

TELECOMMUNICATIONS. (1) Communicating over a distance, as by telegraph or telephone. (2) Any transmission, emission, or reception of signs, signals, writing, images, sounds, or intelligence of any nature by wire, radio, optical, or other electromagnetic systems. (3) The transmission of signals over long distance, such as telegraph, radio, or television.

TYPE SPECIMEN. An individual organism from which the description of a species has been prepared.

USER. In museum registration, a person who utilized the registration system, manual or computerized.

VENUE. The locale of an event or action. Though used most commonly in law, the term *venue* occurs in museology to mean a museum (or other organization, such as a library or private gallery) that hosts a traveling exhibition.

VIDEO DISK. A record-like device capable of storing a large amount of data, both audio and visual, which can be decoded by laser scanner.

WALL TO WALL. A clause in a fine art insurance policy that extends protection from the normal repository (the wall) where shipment originates until it is returned; an important concept because the period of packing and unpacking is automatically insured. The British prefer the term "nail-to-nail."

WOVE PAPER. Paper woven on rollers of tightly meshed wires so as to produce no visible lines running across the grain.

Appendix

Introduction

The *Code of Ethics for Registrars* and the *Code of Practice for Couriering Museum Objects* reflect the work of the professional practices subcommittee of the Registrars Committee of the American Association of Museums (AAM). The subcommittee was aided in its efforts by legal counsel, by considerable contributions from the AAM membership, and by experts from the service industries who work closely with the museum community.

The authors of the *Code of Ethics for Registrars* acknowledge their indebtedness to *Museum Ethics* (American Association of Museums, 1978) and endorse that report as a statement of basic principles applicable to the ethical issues faced by all museum professionals.

The issues surrounding couriering museum objects include the ethics underlying the decision to require a courier and the characteristics, skills, and responsibilities of all parties to the activity—courier, lender, and borrower. The courier is expected to take efficient, rapid, on-site action to preserve museum collections in high-risk, transit situations. The subcommittee intends that the *Code of Practice for Couriering Museum Objects* will provide museum management with standards to evaluate and choose competent couriers.

The subcommittee views the statements in these codes as general guidelines for registrars and for those carrying out the collections management functions normally assigned to a registrar. These codes will be useful in the development of policies and procedures in individual museums. When there are differences of opinion within an institution about practice, registrars may cite the codes to reinforce their position.

The Registrars Committee of the American Association of Museums accepted and endorsed the *Code of Ethics for Registrars* on June 11, 1984; it appeared in *Museum News*, 63, no. 3 (February 1985). The *Code of Practice for Couriering Museum Objects* was accepted and endorsed in June, 1987; it was published in *Registrar*, 4, no. 1.

> Edward Quick, Subcommittee Co-Chair
> Code of Practice for Couriering Museum Objects
>
> Cordelia Rose, Subcommmittee Chair
> Code of Ethics for Registrars

Code of Ethics for Registrars

Description of the Position

Individuals with the title or function of registrar have a varied range of responsibilities and activities. In this document the basic description of the position as defined in the glossary of *Museum Registration Methods* is adopted: "an individual with broad responsibilities in the development and enforcement of policies and procedures pertaining to the acquisition, management and disposition of collections. Records pertaining to the objects for which the institution has assumed responsibility are maintained by the registrar. Usually, the registrar also handles arrangements for accessions, loans, packing, shipping, storage, customs and insurance as it relates to museum material."

Registrars are usually specialists in the areas of information management, risk management, and logistics. The primary concerns of registrars are creating and maintaining accurate records pertaining to objects, including those documents that provide legal protection for their museum; ensuring the safety of objects; arranging insurance coverage for objects; and handling, transporting, and control of objects.

The Registrar, the Records, and the Objects

Registrars' obligations to their museums' collections, to loaned objects and to the associated records are paramount.

MANAGEMENT, MAINTENANCE, AND PRESERVATION OF THE RECORDS

The records and documents that form a body of information pertaining to the collections and loaned objects are the responsibility of registrars and are the cornerstone of the registrarial function.

The records comprise legal documents establishing ownership or loan status of objects: records of accession, location, donor or vendor, exhibition, and publication. They may also include photographs, licenses and permits, exhibition bond notices, and historical records. Frequently, curators keep research files on the objects in their domain.

Registrars must maintain records that are meticulously complete, honest, orderly, retrievable, and current. Records should be created in a timely manner and accurately dated. Records must be stored in an archivally and technologically sound and secure manner, both to ensure their preservation and to prevent access by unauthorized persons. The expertise of legal counsel and archivists should be sought without hesitation.

Registrars must protect their museums and the objects in them against the risk of liability through the use of valid documents such as gift, sales, loan and custody forms and receipts; by implementing all aspects of insurance coverage for owned or borrowed objects on premises or in transit according to the terms of their insurance policy or indemnity; and by complying with pertinent laws and regulations governing such things as import and export or other movement of objects, or rights and reproductions of objects.

Registrars, through the records maintained, are accountable for the objects in the custody of their museums and must be able to provide current information on each object, its location, status, and condition.

MANAGEMENT, MAINTENANCE, AND CONSERVATION OF THE OBJECTS

In maintenance and physical care of the collections, registrars must work in close cooperation with curators, conservators, collections managers, and other museum staff, and must be guided by their museums' collections management policies. In management of loaned objects registrars also work in cooperation with exhibition, technical, and security staff, and they must adhere to and enforce the lenders' conditions of loan.

In some museums it is not registrars but curators or collections managers who have responsibility for the physical care of collections in storage. Whichever is the case, the best and most secure environment possible should be ensured for the storage and preservation of objects. The condition of the collections should be reviewed periodically and the expertise of conservators should be sought without hesitation.

Objects in movement are the responsibility of registrars. As risk managers, registrars are responsible for determining and arranging for the correct methods of handling, packing, transporting, and couriering objects. They must also consider borrowers' capabilities and facilities. Registrars identify potential risks and complications and act to reduce or eliminate them.

Registrars share the responsibilities for loaned objects in the custody of their museums. They are responsible for their safe movement, temporary storage, and correct disposition. Registrars always must treat loaned objects of whatever value, quality, or type with the same care and respect given to objects in their museums' collections.

Registrars must complete condition reports in an honest and timely manner, be familiar with the terms of their insurance coverage and ensure that insurance reporting is accurate. In filing an insurance claim all relevant circumstances of loss or damage must be disclosed, even if it appears that the museum is at fault.

ACQUISITION AND DISPOSAL
Registrars must adhere to the acquisition and disposal policies of their museums; if no written policies exist, then registrars should encourage and assist in their formulation. In the absence of written museum policies registrars should develop written procedures for use by their departments to ensure compliance with traditional but oral museum policies. Registrars should obtain the approval of their directors before implementing such procedures, and strive to ensure that the policies and procedures are complied with at all levels within their museums.

Objects for acquisition or disposal are proposed, usually by curators, to the relevant museum committees for approval. Registrars' roles in acquisition are generally in an advisory capacity concerning the feasibility of storage, the risk of movement to the object under consideration, and certain legal aspects of the transaction. Prior to issuing an accession number reflecting the date and/or order in which the object was added to the collection, registrars are responsible for obtaining documentation of the decision to acquire the object, the document transferring title of an object to the museum, and the receipt of delivery of an object. Registrars should be aware of, and not contribute to, the violation of tax, wildlife, import, or other laws and regulations governing acquisition of objects by their museums and other institutions with which they are involved.

Registrars should ensure that at least one appraisal of an object is acquired and institute insurance coverage if applicable according to museum policy. In order to prevent their use as an appraisal for tax or other purposes, these appraisals should not be made available to the donor or vendor of an object. Appraisals for tax purposes are the responsibility of the donor, who can be informed whether an object is accepted for the collection, for sale, or for use by the museum.

Registrars' roles in deaccessions and disposals are primarily those of monitoring and documenting procedures. Registrars also should bring to the attention of the curator any object in irreparable condition or one jeopardizing the safety of the rest of the collections. Registrars should verify the museum's legal right to dispose of an object, and inform the curator and other appropriate museum staff of any restrictions attached to an object that may bear on its disposition. When restrictions are attached to an object, legal counsel should be sought so that the museum might be relieved of those restrictions by appropriate negotiation or legal procedure.

Once all the proper approvals have been granted, registrars must amend all the related records to show the date of deaccession, the authority for it, and the method of disposal. Records may also show the disposition of any funds realized through sale or any exchange acquired as a result of the deaccession. Donor credit for, and use of funds realized through, the sale of an object must comply with the policies of the museum.

AVAILABILITY OF COLLECTIONS AND RECORDS

Museums hold and safeguard their collections for posterity, although they must allow reasonable public access to them on a nondiscriminatory basis. However, registrars must act according to the policies of their museums.

Registrars, along with curators and conservators, must ensure that objects from the collections are examined and viewed in a manner not detrimental to an object. They must also ascertain that a borrowing institution's facilities are acceptable when considering a loan request, so that an object will not be placed in jeopardy.

The records constitute part of a museum's accountability to the public. However, registrars must ensure by proper supervision that sensitive or confidential material in their museums' records is not accessible to unauthorized persons. When in doubt registrars should consult their supervisors or their museums' legal counsel.

TRUTH IN PRESENTATION

Registrars are responsible for creating and maintaining accurate records and updating them in light of new research, and for ensuring that the records reflect the facts insofar as they are known.

HUMAN REMAINS AND SACRED OBJECTS

Registrars must be tactful and responsible in giving access to collections of human remains and sacred objects, and must store, transport, and care for these objects in a manner acceptable to the profession and to peoples of various beliefs.

Appendix

The Registrar as Staff Member

GENERAL DEPORTMENT

Registrars are visible to the public, the profession, commercial representatives, and government agents in situations ranging from collecting objects from donors and lenders in their homes or museums to negotiating with customs inspectors in cargo sheds. Registrars must behave in a dignified and ethical manner and gain the respect of others by not creating embarrassments either to their museum or their profession. Because of their access to confidential matters and information, it is incumbent upon registrars to be discrete and circumspect in all their communications or actions in an effort to preserve the integrity of their museum.

In all activities and statements, registrars must make it clear whether they are speaking for their museums, their professional association, or themselves. They must be aware that any museum-related action may reflect upon their museums, be attributed to it, or reflect upon the integrity of the profession as a whole.

CONFLICT OF INTEREST

Registrars must be governed by their museums' policies on conflict of interest and other ethical matters.

Registrars should be loyal to their museums and not abuse their official position or contacts within the museum community, nor act so as to impair in any way the performance of their official duties, compete with their museums, or bring discredit or embarrassment to any museum or the profession in any activity, museum-related or not.

RESPONSIBILITY TO THE COLLECTIONS AND OTHER MUSEUM PROPERTY

Registrars and their staff must never receive or purchase for their own or another individual's collections or purposes, even at public auction, objects deaccessioned from their museums' collections. Registrars' volunteers and interns should be guided by the codes governing their supervisors.

Registrars should never put to personal use objects in their museums' custody and they should guard information that would enable others to do so. Registrars must never abuse their access to information and to other museum assets by using them to personal advantage. Registrars must be particularly vigilant concerning their knowledge of museum security procedures.

Because of their experience and responsibility as risk managers, registrars are often regarded as authorities in the care and transport of valuable or problematical objects. They must guard against giving the impression that their museums endorse the services of any specific vendor or supplier.

When recommending the services of conservators, appraisers, packers, shippers, customs brokers, or others, whenever possible registrars should offer the names of three qualified vendors to avoid favoritism in recommendations.

PERSONAL COLLECTING AND DEALING

Registrars must be governed by the policies of their museums which usually are designed for curators and directors. If at the time of their employment their personal collections are similar to those of their museums, registrars should submit an inventory of their collections to the appropriate official and update their inventory in a timely manner. As to objects they acquire after they are employed; registrars may be required to give the museum the opportunity to purchase such objects at their acquisition cost for an appropriate period of time. In no case should registrars compete with their museums in any personal collecting activity. They should never act as dealers or for dealers.

OUTSIDE EMPLOYMENT AND CONSULTING

In any situation where registrars work for another organization, an individual, or themselves on their own time, such work should not interfere with the performance of registrars' duties for their museums. The nature of the employment should be disclosed to and cleared by their director and should conform to their museums' relevant personnel policy.

GIFTS, FAVORS, DISCOUNTS, AND DISPENSATIONS

Registrars often use the services of commercial companies. They must not accept gifts of more than a trifling nature, such as unsolicited advertising or promotional material, so that their judgment will not be impaired when selecting a vendor. Such selections should be made upon merit and not for personal reasons of obligations.

Registrars must not accept personal discounts from vendors who do business with their museums. Registrars must also avoid any appearance of being influenced by gifts or dispensations provided by vendors or services.

TEACHING, LECTURING, WRITING, AND OTHER CREATIVE ACTIVITIES

Registrars should teach, lecture, write, and perform related professional activities for the benefit of others in the profession or those aspiring to such a position. They should also contribute to the general public understanding of museum registration.

Registrars should enhance their own knowledge in all registration matters, ensuring that they are up to date with current methods of records management, object care and handling, packing, transporting, insurance, personnel, and financial management, as well as changes in the laws affecting museums and their collections.

Registrars should obtain the approval of their director and conform to their museums' policies on questions of use of official time, royalties, and other remuneration for such activities.

FIELD STUDIES AND COLLECTING

Because legal and ethical problems can arise more frequently in fieldwork, registrars must be particularly zealous in completing accurate and timely records. Registrars must monitor compliance with local, state, national and international laws, as well as with their museums' acquisitions policies. They must also be sensitive to ethnic or religious beliefs.

The Registrar and Museum Management Policy

PROFESSIONALISM

Although the governing board of the museum is ultimately responsible for the museum, the director is the chief executive officer.

Registrars must carry out their duties according to established guidelines and under the directions of their supervisors, who may be the director, the assistant director, or curator of collections, or an administrative manager. In no case should they take direction from members of the governing board, who should confine their directives to the chief executive officer of the museum. If guidelines or delegations of authority are unclear registrars should seek written clarification.

Registrars should not be required to reverse, alter, or suppress their professional judgment to conform to a management decision.

When a disagreement arises between the registrar and the director or other supervisor, the registrar should consider documenting the difference of opinion, but should also conform to the grievance procedures of the museum. Only when asked to falsify records or in some way compromise legal or ethical standards should the registrar consider writing a report to the governing board of the museum, and then only with the full knowledge of the museum director.

INTERPERSONAL RELATIONSHIPS AND INTERMUSEUM
  COOPERATION

While registrars must strive for excellence in registration methods, they should understand that professional role within the total context of their museum and should act cooperatively and constructively with colleagues in the furtherance of their museums' goals and purposes. It is important for registrars to obtain the respect and trust of colleagues in their own and other museums.

Intermuseum cooperation may take the form of providing safe storage for duplicate sets of collections records, of providing the services of conservation or preparation of objects for transport, of consolidation of shipments or safe storage for traveling exhibitions between sites. Such cooperation may also take the form of providing professional help and temporary storage of objects or records in the event of fire, flood, or other disaster. When objects or records are so taken into their museums' custody, registrars should ensure that valid documentation of the terms and duration of the custody arrangements is provided.

Code of Practice for
Couriering Museum Objects

Courier Policy

The consideration of using a courier is based on certain primary facts, which are that:

Certain museum objects are of a fragile nature, whether by construction or formation, size, materials used, deterioration by age or abuse, and/or require special handling or installation techniques.

Certain museum objects are irreplaceable, rare and unique, politically or culturally sensitive, of extreme artistic, historical, scientific worth, or are of extreme value for other reasons.

Certain shipping routes may prove dangerous to fragile museum objects because such routes expose the object to careless handling, excessive movement, changing and/or extreme temperatures, and other human and/or natural hazards.

Lending and borrowing museums must agree that:

The museum that owns the object may determine that a courier is necessary to lessen the hazards inherent in the object itself, and may specify the transportation method and/or the route to preserve the object from loss by damage or theft and/or to assure that the object will not receive such wear as would cause future problems in the museum's efforts for preservation.

Both the lending and borrowing museum are fully cognizant of and in accord with the limitations and requirements of third parties to the loan (such as insurance companies, transport companies, and forwarding companies) and are in agreement about which museum will take responsibility for actions not covered by such third parties.

The lending and borrowing museums accept that:

The care of museum objects is the top priority in the shipment, except in life-threatening situations.

The requirement of a courier will be established and agreed upon by the lending and borrowing museum by the time the loan agreement is signed and accepted.

The courier, acting as the agent of the lending museum, has full authority to act in protection of the object until the object is officially released to the borrowing museum.

Therefore:

The courier designated must be a museum professional (understanding the condition of the object and its special requirements, familiar with packing, trained in handling, and, as applicable, experienced with transport procedure), in whom the lending museum reposes complete trust for execution of all courier-related duties.

The museum which selects the courier is, in effect, bonding that person for knowledge of the problems of the object and of the transit, for ability to withstand the rigors of travel, and for taking full responsibility for protecting the object.

The courier will be made aware of and understand the responsibilities entrusted to him/her, and of all known or possible hazards which might be encountered in transit.

The lending and borrowing museums must agree in advance on costs related to the courier, on which museum shall pay for them, and on the method of reimbursement for expenses whether foreseen or unforeseen.

The shipment of a museum object will not become the basis for unrelated travel or activity.

Courier Procedures

Who Selects a Courier?

The decision to select a courier should be made in consultation among the director, curator, registrar, and conservator, or by one of these, in accordance with authority specified in museum policy.

Who is Qualified to be a Courier?

Directors, curators, registrars, conservators, and, in certain cases, senior preparators, should be the only people eligible to serve as couriers. People who serve as couriers must be those who are experienced in handling museum objects.

The courier must possess certain qualities: firmness, patience, stamina, and the ability to make intelligent decisions quickly. If the object is to be hand-carried, the courier must have the physical strength to do so. The courier should not carry any luggage while hand-carrying an object. He/she must possess packing skills, be able to make condition reports and effectively use a camera, and be familiar with shippers, brokers, customs, surface transportation, and airport and airline procedures.

Borrower and Lender Agreements and Responsibilities

The agreement to courier an object should be included as part of the loan agreement or a separate written agreement. If the lender has special requirements (that the object be a hand-carry, that it travel flat, that armed guards be required from the door of the aircraft to the door of the museum, that first-class travel is necessary, that an extended stay by the courier at the borrower's institution is required, or special installation instructions) these should be stipulated in writing at the outset. The borrower should clearly outline its courier procedures regarding all flight details or surface arrangements, arrival, unpacking, condition reporting, and installation, as they apply. All arrangements should be understood by all parties well in advance of

241

the shipping date, including back-up plans for sudden schedule changes. Hotel accommodations and terms for daily expenses should be clearly set forth as part of the formal agreement. It is incumbent upon both borrowing and lending museums and their appointed couriers to make every effort to adhere to cost-effective planning and implementation of courier expenses.

Arrangements

The borrowing and lending institution registrars or loan officials make the arrangements for the loan and courier in accordance with accepted practice and the loan agreement.

The registrar or borrower's representative must meet the courier upon delivery. The courier must know exactly where he/she is to be met when arriving. For international shipments, the borrower's customs broker must be at plane-side if possible to supervise off loading while the borrower is bringing the courier to cargo to meet the broker and shipment. The borrower should not move the shipment until the courier is present unless an emergency develops. The borrower's broker must make incoming customs clearance arrangements so that the objects are not jeopardized at the airport by having their crates opened for inspection. The borrower must provide suitable vehicles to get the courier and shipment from the airport to the museum, and provide personnel at the museum to help off load the truck. If courier and object are in separate vehicles they should travel in tandem.

Once the courier is satisfied that the object is safely stored, the borrower should assist the courier in getting to his/her hotel, and should inform the courier how and when to return to the museum to unpack the object. Twenty-four hours should be designated for object acclimatization. The borrower should provide help to unpack, prepare and install the object as necessary, and should initial the courier's condition report.

The borrower must provide secure storage for the courier's objects. The borrower must recognize that the courier has authority over the object until the courier is satisfied with its disposition. The courier should act cooperatively with the borrower's staff and accommodate shipping arrangements and installation schedules.

Accompanied Shipment

An accompanied shipment is one in which a courier agrees to oversee other museum loans in the same shipment, but is not responsible for overseeing packing, unpacking, or making condition reports. Museums and couriers should have a written agreement regarding the accompaniment of their or other objects, clearly stating what the courier is expected to do about other objects, with respect to both responsibility and authority.

Responsibilities of the Courier

The courier constitutes a continuous chain of accountability for the object, from the hands of the lender to those of the borrower. The implication is that the courier can take efficient, rapid, on-site action to preserve the object from, or through, high-risk situations in transit. Secure and expeditious movement of the object can reduce high risk to lower levels of risk.

Responsibilities to the Object

The courier is responsible for witnessing and supervising packing, unpacking after the acclimatization period, transportation, and examination of the object at the beginning and end of shipment.

The courier must stay with the shipment, physically and personally or via constant contact with centers of authority in direct control of the shipment (e.g., customs brokers) where physical presence by the courier is restricted.

The courier must do all that may be necessary to keep delays or possibilities of delays to a minimum. The courier is responsible for anticipating, solving, and reporting unforeseen problems. In the event of a major change in weather, for example, the courier must decide whether it is advisable for the shipment to proceed.

The courier must have no conflicting obligations or reasons

for couriering the object. The courier's family/friends must not travel with the couriered shipment; the courier must not be required nor requested, nor allowed to visit other locations for personal or museum matters before the object is safely delivered; and the schedule of shipment of the object must not be forced to meet appointments nor to ease the courier's trip at the expense of the object.

Skill, Knowledge, and Abilities

The courier must understand and uphold the museum's standards as stated in institution policies. The courier must have vocational knowledge, founded upon practical experience in museums, to understand how these policies relate to "real life" circumstances. The courier must also understand the performance expectations of the borrower.

The courier should join in the pre-evaluation of shipment difficulties: dropped cases, fork-lift hazards, major temperature and humidity variations, palletization and containerization problems (e.g., objects that were wet, excessively heavy, or loose in the container with museum crates), insecure strapping, unscheduled unloading, etc.

The courier must have a knowledge of the object's construction techniques, material, and condition, and must understand the sensitivity of materials and techniques to the varying conditions of transit. He/she must be able to recognize condition problems that require examination or treatment by a conservator.

The courier must know exactly where the object is going, to whom, and by what means, including alternate/back-up routes if schedules are delayed, altered, or cancelled.

The courier should have available from his/her institution or from the borrower:
- a copy of the loan agreement
- business and home addresses, telephone and telex numbers of principals (both borrowers and lenders)
- schedules of transit, including alternates

- insurance restrictions, and a copy of the certificate of insurance
- crate numbers, sizes, weights, and object checklists
- handling instructions
- condition reports
- photograph(s) of the object(s)
- copy of customs invoice

The courier should leave an itinerary with the registrar's office.

The courier should be prepared in advance for delays, cultural differences in conducting business, language barriers, international telephone and telegraphy procedures, possible strikes, and different local and national holidays.

The courier must understand and appreciate the support functions, procedures, restrictions, and authority of carriers, forwarders, customs agents, airport security, lenders and borrowers. The courier must understand the extent of his/her own authority and responsibility, and ascribe neither too little nor too much authority to someone else.

The courier must have a sound knowledge of government regulations that can limit or curtail courier action (e.g., restricted entry).

Information should be given only to priority individuals directly involved in the transit of the object and with a justified need to know. The courier should not tell them anything more than is necessary for them to do their job.

The courier should have some knowledge of shipping, including under-seat sizes, storage areas on board aircraft, and how to seal truck and container locks properly.

The courier must record any container numbers for crated objects, should know position numbers within aircraft, and be seated on the aircraft loading side to watch for unscheduled unloading of crates.

The courier must secure identification of anyone taking crated objects, before releasing the crates. The courier must obtain authorized signature and date on receipts.

The courier must carefully read and understand every document or receipt before signing it, requesting translations when necessary.

The courier must take neither alcohol nor medication that might in any way impair his/her physical mobility and/or ability to make decisions.

The courier should keep accurate accounting of expenses, including copies of all receipts.

Responsibility to the Borrower

The courier must know the borrower's requirements.

The courier is representing his/her institution and as such should conduct himself/herself fairly and ethically:

- The courier should expect to travel coach class unless hand-carrying an object.

- The courier should not make last-minute changes of plan unless essential to the shipment, but if necessary then the borrower should be immediately notified.

- No arrangements should be made that would cause unnecessary risks, complicated timetables, or extra expense.

Bibliography

Registrar's Book Shelf: Suggested Readings

Allen, Carl G., and William B. Allen. "Legal Perils: The Memorandum and Certificate of Insurance." *Museum Insurance Newsletter* (June 1985).

American Association of Museums. *Gifts of Property: A Guide for Donors and Museums*. Washington, D.C: AAM, 1985.

———. *Museum Ethics*, Washington, D.C.: AAM, 1978.

———. *Official Museum Directory*. New York: National Register Publishing Co., Inc., published annually.

American Legal Institute/American Bar Association. *Course of Studies Materials: Legal Problems of Museum Administration*. Philadelphia: ALI/ABA, published annually since 1973.

Association of Art Museum Directors. *Risk Management Manual II*. New York: Association of Art Museum Directors, 1976.

Babcock, Phillip H. "Insurance: Alternatives to Certificates." *Museum News* 57: no. 5 (May/June 1979): 56–57.

Bandes, Susan J., ed. *Caring for Collections: Strategies for Conservation, Maintenance and Documentation*. Washington, D.C.: American Association of Museums, 1984.

Blackaby, James R., Patricia Greeno, and the Nomenclature Committee. *The Revised Nomenclature for Museum Cataloguing: A Revised and Expanded Edition of Robert G. Chenhall's System for Classifying Man-Made Objects*. Nashville: American Association of State and Local History, 1988.

Burke, Robert and Sam Adeloye. *Manual for Basic Museum Security*. Leicestershire, England: Leicestershire Museums for the International Council on Museum Security, 1986.

Cannon-Brookes, Peter. "A Draft Code of Practice for Escorts and Couriers." *The International Journal of Museum Management and Curatorship* (March 1982).

Chenhall, Robert G. *Museum Cataloguing in the Computer Age.* Nashville: American Association for State and Local History, 1978.

Chenhall, Robert G., and Peter Homulos. "Museum Data Standards." *Museum News* 56: no. 6 (July/August 1978): 43–48.

Doloff, F. and R. Perkinson. *How to Care for Works of Art on Paper.* Boston: Museum of Fine Arts, 1971.

Dudley, Dorothy H., Irma Bezold Wilkinson et al. *Museum Registration Methods.* Washington, D.C.: American Association of Museums, 1979.

Estes, Carol, and Keith W. Sessions, eds. *Controlled Wildlife, A Three-Volume Guide to U.S. Wildlife Laws and Permit Procedures.* Lawrence, Kansas: Association of Systematics Collections, 1983.

Fall, Frieda Kay. *Art Objects, Their Care and Preservation: A Handbook for Museums and Collectors.* La Jolla, California: Lawrence McGilvery, 1973.

Feldman, Franklin and Stephen E. Weil with Susan Duke Biederman. *Art Law.* 2 vols. Boston: Little, Brown and Company, 1986.

Fennelly, Lawrence J. *Museum Archive and Library Security.* Boston: Butterworth, 1983.

Gallery Association of New York State with The Metropolitan Museum of Art, Division of Educational Services. *Insurance and Risk Management for Museums and Historical Societies.* Hamilton, New York: Gallery Association of New York State, 1985.

Gould, D.A. *Crate Specifications.* Washington, D.C.: Smithsonian Institution Traveling Exhibition Service, 1975.

Harris, Cyril M. and Charles F. Crede, eds. *Shock and Vibration Handbook.* New York: McGraw Hill, 1976.

Hilberry, John D. and Susan Kalb Weinberg. "Museum Collections Storage." Parts I, II, III. *Museum News* 59: no. 5 (March/April 1981): 7–21; no. 6 (May/June 1981): 5- 23; no. 7 (July/August 1981): 49–60.

Hoachlander, Marjorie E. *Profile of a Museum Registrar.* Washington, D.C.: Academy for Educational Development, 1979.

Horne, Stephen A. *Way to Go!: Crating Artwork for Travel.* Hamilton, New York: Gallery Association of New York State, 1985.

Keck, Caroline K. *A Handbook on the Care of Paintings.* Nashville: American Association for State and Local History, 1967.

Keck, Caroline K., Huntington T. Block, Joseph Chapman, John B. Lawton, and Nathan Stolow. *A Primer on Museum Security.* Cooperstown, New York: New York State Historical Association, 1974.

Lee, Welton, Bruce M. Bell, and John F. Sutton, eds. *Guidelines for Acquisition and Management of Biological Specimens.* Lawrence, Kansas: Association of Systematics Collections, 1982.

Light, Richard B., Andrew D. Roberts, and Jennifer D. Stewart, eds. *Museum Documentation Systems: Developments and Applications.* Boston: Butterworth, 1986.

Lusk, Carroll B. "The Invisible Danger of Invisible Light." *Museum News* 58: no. 2 (November/December 1979): 22–23.

Malaro, Marie C. "Collections Management Policies." *Museum News* 58: no. 2 (November/December 1979): 57–61.

———. *A Legal Primer on Managing Museum Collections.* Washington, D.C.: Smithsonian Institution Press, 1985.

MacCleish, A. Bruce, ed. *The Care of Antiques and Historical Collections.* 2 ed. Nashville: American Association of State and Local History, 1985.

Mason, Donald. *The Fine Art of Art Security: Protecting Public and Private Collections Against Theft, Fire, Vandalism.* New York: Van Nostrand Reinhold Co., 1979.

"Museums and Computers." *Museum News* 50: no. 1 (September 1971): entire issue.

"Museums and Computers." *Museum News* 56: no. 3 (January/February 1978): entire issue.

Museum Data Bank Committee. *Museum Data Bank Research Report Series.* Rochester, New York: Museum Data Bank Committee, 1974–77.

Nauert, Patricia, ed. *Registrar's Report,* 1977–1979. Each of nine issues devoted to a different topic of interest to registrars.

Copies may be obtained by sending $1 per issue and a self-addressed, stamped envelope to R. Montgomery, L.A. County Art Museum, 5905 Wilshire Blvd., Los Angeles, California.

———. *Reg Tech: A Workbook for a Seminar in Museum Registration Techniques.* Los Angeles: Museum Associates of the Los Angeles County Museum of Art, 1975.

Nauert, Patricia, and Carolyn M. Black. *Fine Arts Insurance: A Handbook for Art Museums.* Savannah, Georgia: Association of Art Museum Directors, 1979; distributed by the American Association of Museums, Washington, D.C.

Perry, Kenneth D., ed. *Museum Forms Book.* Austin, Texas: Texas Association of Museums, 1980.

Phillimore, Elizabeth. *A Glossary of Terms Useful in Conservation: With a Supplement on Reporting the Condition of Antiquities.* Ottawa: Canadian Museums Association, 1976.

Piechota, Dennis V., and Gretta Hansen. "The Care of Cultural Property in Transit: A Case Design for Traveling Exhibitions." *Technology and Conservation* (Winter) 1982, 32–46.

Registrars Committee of the American Association of Museums. *Registrar.* Spring 1984—.

Reibel, Daniel B. *Registration Methods for the Small Museum: A Guide for Historical Collections.* Nashville: American Association for State and Local History, 1978.

Richoux, Jeannette A., Jill Serota-Braden, and Nancy Demyttenaere. "A Policy for Collections Access." *Museum News* 59: no. 7 (July/August 1981): 43–47.

Sarasan, Lenore. "Why Museum Computer Projects Fail." *Museum News* 59: no. 4 (January/February 1981): 40–49.

Sarasan, Lenore, and A. M. Neuner, comps. *Museum Collections and Computers: Report of an ASC Survey.* Lawrence, Kansas: Association of Systematics Collections, 1983.

Solley, Thomas T., Joan Williams, Linda Baden, *Planning for Emergencies: A Guide for Museums.* Washington, D.C.: American Association of Museum Directors, 1987.

Stolow, Nathan. *Conservation and Exhibitions: Packing, Transport, Storage and Environmental Considerations.* Boston: Butterworth, 1987.

Thomson, Garry. *The Museum Environment.* Boston: Butterworth, 1986.

Tillotson, Robert G. *Museum Security.* Paris: International Council of Museums, with the assistance of the American Association of Museums, 1977.

Ullberg, Alan D. and Pegram Epes. "The Museum Registrar and the New American Association of Museums Ethics Code." *Registrar's Report* 1: no. 8 (1979).

Wilcox, U. Vincent. "Collections Management with the Computer." *Curator* 23: no. 1 (1980): 43–54.

Witteborg, Lothar P. and Andrea P. Stevens, eds. *Good Show! A Practical Guide for Temporary Exhibitions.* Washington, D.C.: Smithsonian Institution Traveling Exhibition Service, 1981.

Zuboff, Shoshana. *In the Age of the Smart Machine.* New York: Basic Books, Inc., 1988.

Photographic Credits

Photographic Credits

Cover: Anonymous, *Seated Scribe,* Egyptian, 1554/1305 BC, basalt, 2½ inches, 31.70. Gift of Mrs. Lillian Henkel Haass and Miss Constance Haass. Photograph courtesy of the Founders Society, Detroit Institute of Arts.

Page 2: Photograph courtesy of the Fine Arts Museums of San Francisco.

Page 12: Photograph courtesy of Mary Randlett, photographer, Seattle.

Page 34: Photograph courtesy of the National Gallery of Art, Washington.

Page 46: John F. Peto, *Old Companions,* 1904, oil on canvas, 22 × 30 inches. Collection of Jo Ann and Julian Ganz, Jr.

Page 58: Photograph courtesy of the Smithsonian Institution, Washington. Joan Andrews, photographer.

Page 76: Detail of Victor Higgins, *Pueblo of Taos,* oil on canvas, 43½ × 53½ inches, the Anschutz Collection, Denver. Milmore, photographer.

Page 90: Photograph courtesy of Artech, Fine Art Services, Seattle. Jim Ball, photographer.

Page 112: Photograph courtesy of The American Federation of Arts, New York.

Page 130: *The Works of Mr. William Shakespeare* . . . Revised and corrected by N. Rowe, Esq., 1709, Henry VI, frontispiece. Photograph courtesy of The Folger Shakespeare Library, Washington.

Page 144: Photograph courtesy of the National Gallery of Art, Washington.

Page 160: Photograph courtesy of the Louisiana State Museum, New Orleans. Michael Palumbo, photographer.

Page 174: Photograph courtesy of the Library of Congress, Washington.

Page 178: George Caleb Bingham, *Boatmen on the Missouri,* 1846, oil on canvas, 25½ by 30⅜ inches, 1979.7.15. Gift of Mr. and Mrs. John D. Rockefeller 3rd. Photograph courtesy of the Fine Arts Museums of San Francisco.

Page 186: Probe wires of test equipment radiate from silicon chip holding the smallest transistors in the world. Photograph courtesy of the IBM Corporation.

Page 194: Computer reconstruction obtained from axial computed tomography (CT) data showing how the three thousand year old Egyptian mummy Ta-bes would look if unwrapped. Photograph courtesy of Myron Marx, Pacific Presbyterian Medical Center, San Francisco.

Page 206: Interior, Museum Support Center. Photograph courtesy of the Smithsonian Institution, Washington. Dane Penland, photographer.